Born-Again

VIRGIN

How To Transform Your Life From

Promiscuity Back Into Purity

By Vilma Conner

MIRACON

ENTERPRISES

Published by
Miracon Enterprises
P.O. Box 250577
Glendale, CA 91225
www.miraconenterprises.com

ISBN 978-0-9823316-0-6

Printed in the United States of America.

*This book is dedicated to all of the women in the
Los Angeles Dream Center Discipleship program –
past, present, and future. You all are my heroes!
Your desire to change and pursuit after God
gives me the motivation in life.
Thank you all for being the guinea pigs
for the exercises I use throughout this book.
You ladies have a very special place in my heart!*

Acknowledgements

__Jesus Christ__ -Turning my life over to him was the best decision I made in my entire life! He's always been faithful. He loved me even when I didn't love myself. Jesus, the lover of my soul, inspired me to write this book to help other single adults who struggle with the same things I did.

__Mike__ –Thank you for all your support and for believing in me. You showed me how to love again even with all my hurts and mistakes from past relationships. I am blessed beyond measure with the best husband anyone could ever ask for!

__Sherrie__-You showed me how to be affectionate with women without getting all freaked out. I appreciate your loyalty. *__Lorna__*-Thank you for being that spiritual mentor to me. Your love for hurting people showed me how to love hurting people, too. *__Ida__*-Thank you for being that pillar of strength. I enjoy analyzing life and people with you. *__Joyce__*-Thank you for all the memories of adventuring the inner city of Los Angeles together. The trip to the Staples center topped them all. *__Kaci__*-All I have to say is…those were the days. Keep the faith ladies. The best is yet to come! I love you all!

CONTENTS

INTRODUCTION: *"What is a Born-Again Virgin?"* 9

PART I - *ABC's of the Single Life*

    ABC 19

1. ACCOUNTABILITY 27

2. BOUNDARIES 39

3. COMMITMENT 55

4. X-RAY VISION 61

5. YOUR THOUGHTS 69

6. ZEALOUS ATTITUDE 87

PART II - *Recess Break*

7. SABBATICAL 95

8. DWELL IN IT OR DEAL WITH IT 109

9. POTENTIAL PROSPECT 127

10. UNDER GOD'S CONSTRUCTION 139

11. BEAUTY FOR ASHES 153

PART III - *Ready, Set, GO!*

12. DON'T WORRY, BE HAPPY 167

13. REPORT CARD 179

14. THE POINT OF "KNOW" RETURN 187

15. GRADUATION 195

"I will build you up again

and you will be rebuilt,

O VIRGIN…"

Jeremiah 31:4

INTRODUCTION

"What Is A Born-Again Virgin?"

Come on a journey with me to discover what it means to be a Born-Again Virgin. The question I always get from people is, "How is it possible to be a virgin-AGAIN?" Once you lose your virginity, you can't get it back. Can you? Ponder with me for a moment Nicodemus in Chapter 3 of the book of John, Jesus was speaking about being born-again. Nicodemus ask, "How can a man be born [again] when he is old?" This scripture teaches that because of God's love, you can start life over again just like a new-born baby. This includes your sexual life.

Any male or female who is a child of God can become a Born-Again Virgin. Being a Christian is the first half of the equation. The second half of the equation is restoring your identity as a virgin in God's eyes. The Bible says in **Isaiah 1:18 – "though your sins are like scarlet, they shall be as white as snow,**

though they are red as crimson, they shall be like wool." God will wash away your wrongdoings (sins) and this will make you clean again.

God has laid it on my heart to write this book for those who have lived a worldly life style before getting saved. I was living by the world's standards until I became a Christian. Little did I know that when I was born-again, my slate would be wiped clean and I would get to start all over again. This makes me a Born-Again Virgin - maybe not scientifically, but emotionally and spiritually. The Word of God says in **2 Corinthians 5:17 – "Therefore, if anyone is in Christ, he is a new creation; the old has gone, the new has come!"**

My Born-Again Virgin journey started when I got this revelation from God in the middle of a mission trip in Jamaica. A prophet told me he saw me in a really, really, *really* white wedding dress with a headpiece but no veil. In my carnal mind, I thought, **YES!** He is prophesying that I will be getting married soon, but when I spoke, what came out of my mouth was shocking because it wasn't what was in my thoughts. When the prophet asked me what this meant to me, I told him that the reason he saw me in a very white wedding dress was because God had given me back my purity! My slate was clean and I was as white as snow. The reason I didn't have a veil covering my face was because I had nothing to hide anymore. My past was history and I didn't have to hide my face behind a veil because I had nothing to be ashamed of. That's when I realized I became a Born-Again Virgin.

As a born-again Christian, I learned how to live a whole new spiritual life. It's just like when I was a kid in school. I needed to learn my ABC's before I could learn to read and write. It's the same way with being a Born-Again Virgin. I had to learn God's roadmap for my new life journey, especially in the area of singleness.

The Bible has rules to live by for your safety and well-being. I didn't know this when I first got saved. I thought these rules were stopping me from having fun. I didn't know what healthy relationships were. I thought as long as I didn't have sex with someone that it was a healthy relationship. I thought I was mature enough to handle one-on-one time with the opposite sex. After all, I was an adult with plenty of experience in relationships. The first time I heard the term "group dating", I thought it was a corny Christian rule that socially awkward people made up because they couldn't carry on conversations with the opposite sex.

It wasn't until I became involved in a singles ministry that I realized that the dating rules for Christians are different from the world's rules. The only rule that guided my choices before I became a Christian was, "If it feels good and you are not hurting anyone, just do it". The famous quote, *"JUST DO IT"* reigns in today's single society.

If you are coming out of the lifestyle of the world, you might struggle with the Christian concept of relationships. The rules aren't meant to stop you from having fun. These rules for Christian singles are meant to protect you and to give you the abundant life that Jesus promises in **John 10:10 "...I have come that they may have life, and have it to the full"**. What the world considers pleasurable is only temporary. What the bible considers as pleasurable is everlasting. Finding true pleasure only happens if it is done God's way.

It is my hope that this book will be a great challenge to you in restoring and redefining your life in the area of singleness. Throughout the book there are "Time-Out" sections for you to take a moment and reflect on that issue. Some time-outs will direct you to a website to get more information regarding that specific topic. On the website, go to the book entry menu. Then enter the keyword you will get from the "Time-Out" section. There are no right or wrong answers. Let the Holy Spirit lead you in what the right response is for you. These questions and exercises will assist you in understanding more about yourself, your relationships with others and God.

You've probably heard this saying before, "What you put into it is what you will get out of it". If you just read this book, then you will not get much out of it. But if you take some of these principles and apply them to your single life, you will get more out of this book. Most importantly you will get more out of life.

I pray that this book will help you live life to the fullest as a Born-Again Virgin! Let it reveal godly ways to guide you in your struggles with singleness and relationships. **Psalm 19:8 says, "The precepts of the LORD are right, giving joy to the heart. The commands of the LORD are radiant, giving light to the eyes".** By obeying his commands, your eyes will be opened that will bring joy to your heart. May the contents of this book open your eyes and bring joy to your heart as a Christian single adult.

Some of you will be hearing this for the first time. For others, it will be a refresher for you. Just sit back and open up your heart. Let the Holy Spirit be your Teacher and Counselor when it comes to relationships. May every single one of you receive a personal revelation from God that you can enjoy the journey to the fullest during your season of singleness. That is what life is all about. Are you ready for your Born-Again Virgin journey? If you are, let's get started by getting back to the basics.

Time-Out #1

Check to see if you are ready for this journey on the website below:

 Internet Interactive Website: **www.bavirgin.com**

Book Entry Keyword: **START**

Vilma Conner

PART I

ABC's of the Single Life

ABC

Every journey has a starting point. It's the beginning of something new. You need to start off with the basics. When people join the military, they must go through basic training to know what to do before they are released out in the field. If they don't have the basic training, there is no way they can survive out there. It is the same way in learning the basics of the single life as a Born-Again Virgin. If you can learn the basics in the beginning of this journey, it will help you survive out in the single's field.

You might be a brand new Christian and all of this is new to you. Maybe you were raised in a Christian home. There are different churches with many different traditions, practices and beliefs. Even though our stories are different, we are all part of the same human race.

This book is for any single man or woman interested in living life to the fullest as a Christian. Men will be able to apply the principles from this book to their lives. However, to make things flow better with my life story, it will be focus more towards single women.

This may be your first book about being single or you may have a bookshelf full of self-help books. Whether this is your first book or a refresher, you need to hear about being single God's way, not the world's way or your own way. The Bible is the foundation in basic training for Born-Again Virgins, providing a secure platform to stand on.

Everyone needs to have a bible verse for life that has personal meaning and purpose. This will help you keep your focus on your journey! Find a verse that is unique to you that God lays on your heart. My life scripture is Proverbs 3:5. Over the years, I have learned and still continue to learn to trust God with every area in my life. When I don't lean on my own understanding, he shows me his way with various situations in my life. This

Trust in the Lord with all your heart and lean not on your own understanding; in all your ways acknowledge him, and He will make your path straight.

Proverbs 3:5,6

scripture is so precious to me that I have a ring that is inscribed with Proverbs 3:5. This is my wedding band to God. I've always worn it on my right hand because I wanted to make sure people knew I was single with my left ring finger still available. As a single adult, I wanted to make sure that finger was open for a wedding ring. Can I get an Amen to that?

Throughout my Born-Again Virgin journey, this life scripture has gotten me through the hard times of being single. Without understanding the Bible, you will not survive this journey. Let's take a moment to find out where understanding comes from.

Have you read more worldly books and/or magazines than Christian ones? If you have, you are leaning on your own understanding and attaining knowledge by the world's standards. Many people (including Christians) read more worldly books and magazines regarding dating and relationships than Christian books based on the Bible. These worldly books often have surveys regarding sex, relationships and what men/women really want, etc. I've been there and done that! I thought it couldn't hurt me because I just wanted to learn more about relationships, men and myself. That is the first mistake I made. Going to the secular world for answers is not the answer for Christians. In Hosea 4:6 God says, "My people are destroyed from lack of knowledge".

Some people are failing in the area of relationships because of not being informed properly. Where did you learn about sex? Maybe your parents tried to tell you about the birds and the bees in kindergarten. Or perhaps, you had to go to a sex class in middle school. Like many of us, you might also learn from TV, magazines, friends or even experimentation. There are so many classes such as English, Physical Education, and even Home Economics to help us prepare for life, but very little on dating, relationships and sexuality. No wonder young people struggle in this area today!

The World's way is all about me, myself, and I. Like a fast food restaurant once said, *"Have it your way"*. But this is not God's way. God's way is higher and better than our ways. Having it your way takes you down the road of destruction. Think about it. So far, where has your way gotten you? Even the devil can deceive the church. Many churches will not open up and talk about sex at the pulpit for this is taboo. So where are Christian singles to go for answers? If the church will not talk about it, they have no other choice than to go to the world. Christians are being destroyed by the world, the devil and even themselves from the lack of godly knowledge that can only come from the Bible.

You are all probably thinking what I used to think when I was single. Why is someone who is *married* teaching about being single and relationships? She doesn't understand where I'm at because she is already married. **WRONG,** I was there for over 15 years of my adult life! That equals 180 months or 780 weeks or 5,400 days or 8,760 hours that I had to wait until I got married. So, I *DO* understand the single life journey. Why do you think I wrote this book? I know how difficult it is.

Let me take you back in time. I remember when I finally got tired of the single life of doing whatever felt good, drinking, partying, and going out to bars.

Hangovers and one night-stands were a big let down after years of trying to find Mr. Right. I thought to myself, surely there has to be some decent guys in this world, but where can they be? The first thought that came to mind was church. Certainly guys that went to church had to be decent. So I decided to go to a single's service to meet guys and I found the most decent guy ever – Jesus! Now, becoming born-again did not mean that my old habits were changed instantly. Even to this day, I have to seek wisdom continually and alter my life to God's will. I will talk more about this in the "Recess Break" section of this book.

During those years of struggling with being single, I cried more than the people around me knew. I got depressed and even upset with God for not bringing me a husband. However, it was in these times that my relationship with God was the most intimate. My family couldn't help me. My married friends couldn't help me. My single friends could relate to me, but we would end up down in the dumps together and that would depress me even more. So I would sit at home alone and have my own "pity party" all by myself. The only thing that I could do was cry out to God when I was lonely. There were even times when I would throw a fit and tell God off. But he never failed to comfort me and embrace me with his love, even when I didn't want it. Then when I was done with my "pity party", I would feel really bad and have to apologize to God. But that is okay because he can handle my little fits. I believe God wants us to be completely honest with him about our feelings and emotions. Being real with him all the time is part of having a relationship with him.

When you are lonely and there seems to be emptiness in your heart that usually means you need to spend more time with Jesus. Even when you have a mate in your life you will still feel lonely at times. I know some people that are lonelier being married than when they were single. Why is that? Because they were looking to another person to give them joy in their lives. Having an intimate relationship with God is the most important step to attaining true satisfaction in every other relationship.

I've found for myself, my friends and other Christian single adults I have counseled, that a few simple ABC's of relationships can help you on your journey as a Born-Again Virgin. Let's continue our basic training together, shall we?

1

ACCOUNTABILITY

"Involving Others In Your Life"

You might cringe when you hear the word accountability. You might think that means letting people get up in your personal business. To some extent, that is true. However, it's up to each individual how much to let someone else in. Even Jesus had others involved in his life. He and the disciples had each other for accountability.

The word accountability means being accountable to someone. The dictionary definition is "an obligation or willingness to accept responsibility or to account for one's actions".[i] This is probably the most

So then, each of us will give an account of himself to God.

important component in learning the basics of being a Born-Again Virgin. It's a requirement.

The word accountability is not in the Bible, however, the word account is. There will come a day when you will stand before God and give an account for everything that you have done on this earth. This includes simple things such as what comes out of your mouth as stated in Matthew 12:36, "But I tell you that men will have to give account on the day of judgment for every careless word they have spoken".

Wow! When I think of how often I say stupid things to others, exaggerate or even lie, it makes me realize how much I need accountability in my life. When I stand before God on that day, I will have no excuse for my actions or words. So what can be done right here, right now?

First, you cannot lean on your own understanding and try to do it all by yourself. How many times do you make bad decisions when you know better? Yet, you make them anyways because your flesh over-rides your spirit. If you do it on your own, you will fail. It's true that you need the Holy Spirit to help, but you also need the help of people you trust to speak into your life.

If you are like me, wisdom goes out the window when I find myself in a relationship. Even when I hear the Holy Spirit speaking to me, I tend to ignore Him. So I need that extra audible help from someone I trust to keep me in my right mind when I cannot do it myself.

Surrounding yourself with people who are trustworthy and who have your best interest at heart is crucial. These people make great accountability partners. The definition of an accountability partner is one that will join you in action. That means someone that will keep you accountable to your actions. It is important that you find the right person. Not everyone, particularly your friends, will make good accountability partners.

There can be different accountability partners for different things to help you on your journey. For example, you may have one accountability partner to keep you accountable in your spiritual walk, and yet another to keep you accountable in relationships. However, if you choose too many accountability partners, you might be tempted to go to certain ones looking for the answer you know will justify what you are doing. Plus, you may tell one thing to one and not the other or forget whom you told what to. The key is to communicate, communicate, and then communicate some more to your accountability partners.

Let's look at finding the right types of accountability partners. Start with people you know are strong in their walk with the Lord. When selecting an accountability partner, find someone that will truly hold you accountable. This should be someone that is spiritually mature and has high relationship standards. This does not mean a friend who will tell you everything you want to hear, supports you with whatever decision you make, and never challenges or

...Speaking the truth in Love...
Ephesians 4:15

questions you. You know these types of friends. Even though they may be your good friends or even best friends, they most likely will not be good accountability partners.

Mature Christians, church leaders, pastors or even Christian parents will make great accountability partners. These are people you trust that will speak the truth in love, whether it's what you want to hear or not. Make sure that your accountability partner is the same sex as you. Ladies, you should never have a male accountability partner and vice-versa, men should never have a female accountability partner. This could be a dangerous situation. Affairs can start off this way.

Start by writing down a few potential people that you think would be good accountability partners. Put down their qualities and why they would make good accountability partners for you. Pray and ask God to help you choose the one that would be best for you. Next, write down when you will go to them and the things that you want them to keep you accountable to. Below is an outline to be used in selecting an accountability partner.

Time-Out #2

ACCOUNTABILITY PARTNER SELECTION:

Potential Partners:

1. _____

2. _____

3. _____

Qualities:

1. _____

_____

_____

2. _____

_____

_____

3. _____

_____

_____

Best Choice: _____

Explain Why: _____

_____

_____

_____

My Accountability Partner(s) will be:

_____

_____

_____

I will go to them when I...

➢ _____

_____

➢ _____

_____

➢ _____

_____

They will help me with...

➢ _____

_____

➢ _____

_____

➢ _____

_____

After completing the accountability partner outline, ask the first person on your list if he/she would like to be your accountability partner. That person may say no, so then you ask the next person on your list of potentials. When you find the right accountability partner, make an agreement with that person.

This agreement should state what is expected from her and what is expected from you. Being realistic is a must. Always seal your agreement with the Holy Spirit as your witness.

The following is an agreement for you and your accountability partner to use. Let me suggest that you finish reading this entire book prior to filling out this accountability partner agreement. This book will give you more insight into the terms and conditions of your accountability partner agreement.

To download a FREE copy of the Accountability Partnership Agreement, go to the website below:

Internet Interactive Website: **www.bavirgin.com**

Book Entry Keyword: ACCOUNTABILITY

ACCOUNTABILITY PARTNERSHIP AGREEMENT

THIS AGREEMENT, entered into this _____ day of _____ 20_____ by
and between _____ hereinafter participant
and
_____hereinafter partner.

TERMS AND CONDITIONS:

1.   **Confidentiality:** partner will keep confidentiality unless participant
     breaks any legal laws, rules for grounds of agreement termination, or a threat
     to themselves (participant). The partner has the obligation to confront the
     participant. If participant does not receive what partner is saying, the partner
     will practice Matthew 18:15-20 in bringing a third party to help the participant.

2.   **Honesty:** participant will be very open and honest with the accountability
     partner regarding any interest in a person, boundaries, thoughts, and
     struggles the participant is having. Partner will not judge or criticize anything
     that the participant may say or do. Partner will speak words of
     encouragement from the bible, speak the truth in love even if it means being
     firm and strong with convictions from the word of God.

3.   **Status:** participant will continually check in regularly, with the partner to
     give updates on their progress. Partner has the permission to ask personal
     questions and will continue to give guidance and encouragement to
     participant.

ADDITIONAL TERMS & CONDITIONS: _____
_____
_____
_____

SIGNED IN THE PRESENCE OF:

The Holy Spirit
_____
Witness

_____
Participant   Date

_____
Partner   Date

You must always be open and honest with your accountability partners. Let them know when you have an interest in someone, even if it's just a hint of interest. Share with them the boundaries (we'll talk more about this in the next chapter) that you have set for your relationships. Your accountability partner can help you see when you are headed towards stepping over boundaries you have made. Check in regularly with your accountability partner to give updates on where you are with new interests or relationships.

When you are interested in someone, you will want to spend time with that person. Some people feel safe if they are in a group of three so that there is a chaperone. A chaperone for a date is not necessarily a bad thing. I remember when I was a teenager and whenever I went on a date, I had to take my little brother with me. I hated him going but as I looked back, it kept my date and I from making out and being physical. We had to keep the date G-rated since my little brother was present. Plus, my brother would tell my dad everything that we did on the date. I didn't realize it back then, but he was somewhat of an accountability partner.

Having a chaperone may prevent you from being too physical but it does not prevent you from getting emotionally attached. You can still get attached to someone with others around. To prevent getting too close to someone physically or emotionally, you must have group accountability. A group date consists of at least five or more people, without being coupled off. If you bring a friend who wants to come because she's interested in one of the guys who will be there, she probably won't notice what you're doing with the guy you are interested in.

There is safety in numbers, but you still have to choose wisely or you might find yourself getting too intimate too soon. Group dating also gives you the opportunity to see how the person you're interested in treats others. This could give you valuable insight as to how that person will treat you if you become involved. Church functions, home groups or community events are all great choices for group accountability.

2

<u>B</u>OUNDARIES

"Smart Surroundings"

Look at the walls in your house. These walls are there to keep you inside where you are safe and secure. The walls also keep people out that you don't want in with you. In the same sense, a boundary is to keep something in or keep something out. Boundaries in relationships are there to set a limit in keeping the right things in and the wrong things out.

God places boundaries in our lives to keep us safe. Boundaries even go back to the beginning with Adam and Eve. The only boundary they had was not to eat from a certain tree. Why was that boundary set for them? It was to protect them and keep them from sinning.

At first, boundaries may appear harsh or controlling. In actuality, they provide the framework for you to become your personal best. It will protect you from heartaches, hurts, disappointments and bad consequences from wrong relationships. As a Born-Again Virgin, you must set boundaries in the areas of time, emotions and physical touch.

TIME: Too much time spent in deep conversation about relationships, personal issues, sexuality, etc. is the beginning of danger. Talking for hours on the phone can be more intimate than you realize. I've been there and done that, too! Have you ever NOT BEEN interested in someone in the beginning, but as you have deeper conversations with that person, you start seeing them in a different light. Then all of the sudden, that person becomes "The One" to you. Without boundaries, you might give into spending too much time with one person and quickly go down the wrong path. Boundaries help you stay on the right path on your Born-Again Virgin journey.

Before jumping into a relationship, you MUST watch to see how that person of interest interacts with others. By watching and observing from a distance, you will be able to see potential problems such as anger problem or an abusive behavior. See how they treat their family members. If you don't take a step back, your intellect gets clouded. If you jump into something too soon, you will compromise in a lot of areas because you will only see the good in that person. Everything else will be ignored.

I remember I had this guy that I was infatuated with because I thought he was "The One". This is just one of "The Ones" I thought for sure was "The One". On the outside he was handsome, physically fit, he had a good job, owned his own home, and was a Christian. He was everything I thought I wanted…until I saw him in a group setting. He became very possessive of me. He didn't mingle with others. He would only talk to me and didn't like me talking to other guys. It blew me away because he was very different when we talked for hours on the phone. He portrayed himself as being very friendly and talked about being a social butterfly. Until I saw him in action, I believed his description of himself. Come to find out later, he was controlling and obsessive in other dating relationships, too.

When it comes to setting boundaries with your time, you must limit the amount of time on the phone or even in person. Let that person know in the beginning that you have boundaries set with every type of relationship, including friendships. This way there are no misunderstandings. You can recall the boundaries you set in the beginning if that person start crossing over them. In the beginning of a relationship, you want to get to know that person as a friend first. If you start viewing that individual as anything other than a friend, your initial intention is not pure which will lead you down the wrong path.

If you talk to someone every day, especially on the phone, you are spending too much time with that particular person. If you talk on the phone or one-on-one in person for over 30 minutes, you are spending too much time with that person. Think about it, how often do you spend talking to an acquaintance? In the beginning, everyone should only be an acquaintance for a period of time before getting to know them as a friend. During this time, there shouldn't be too much personal conversation being exchanged.

Another thing to consider is that if you spend more time talking and/or spending time with a person other than with God, then you are putting that person above God. If you do this, you are making this person an idol and you have broken a boundary set by God. Idolatry is one of the Ten Commandments in the Bible (see Exodus 20).

Boundaries with time are critical in the beginning stages of any relationship. Ask yourself if God would be pleased by the long conversations you have with this particular person. I know those conversations are not always glorifying to God. It may start out with good intentions talking about God, but the more you talk to one particular person, it turns far away from that. It can eventually lead to sexual talk.

EMOTIONS: It is easy to act according to your emotions; especially if you think something will make you feel good. It is not easy to control emotions. However, the Bible states in **Proverbs 4:23, "Above**

all else, GUARD your heart for it is the wellspring of life." This is a MUST in being a Born-Again Virgin!

I had to say a prayer daily for God to GUARD my heart from all the guys the devil threw at me. I didn't want anyone interested in me unless it was my mate for life. Do you know that God did just that? Each time I became interested in someone, something always came up whether it was that guy was totally clueless, moved away or started dating someone else. I would get mad, but God would gently bring to my remembrance the three things I prayed about regarding guys:

GOD, PLEASE...

1. Guard my heart
2. Not my will, but Yours be done
3. Give my heart to my mate because I always gave my heart out to the wrong guys. *(The choices I made usually ended up hurting me)*

You need to concentrate on those emotions that will keep you on the right path. You need to look straight ahead, keep your eyes fixed on God, and not go on detours that lead to sin. The most important thing to remember is that you do have control over your emotions. You need to learn to rule them rather than allowing them to rule you. This is done by setting emotional boundaries.

You must be able to identify and describe your emotions. Choose family, friends and significant adults that are able to discuss your emotions with you. Choose someone that has known you for a long period of time and will be truthful with you. Ask them to be honest about what makes you emotional and how you re-act to certain situations. Once you know what sets you off, you must go to your accountability partner to help you keep emotional boundaries in place.

For example, if like many women, you're having one of those days when you feel ugly and you need compliments from others. Your tendency is to go to the opposite sex to boost your ego by flirting with them. This behavior can get you into trouble when it's that time of the month and your emotions are out of whack. Instead, go to your accountability partner and share how you are feeling.

Controlling your emotions with boundaries will help you NOT to act on them. If you start feeling like your emotions are acting up, call your accountability partner and let them know what is making you feel this way. Talk it through with someone that will uphold you in this area. Let me remind you, it should NEVER BE with the opposite sex. You are only asking for trouble when you go to the opposite sex for emotional comfort. Women especially need to go to other women for emotional comfort. Have them pray for you. This will eventually pass. You just need a little help and encouragement in getting you through this emotional struggle.

PHYSICAL: This could be the most hazardous boundary if it is broken. Setting physical boundaries is a MUST to survive your journey of a Born-Again Virgin. If you have been sexually active before being born-again, you must be real and know – "How far is too far" for you. Some people are okay with a kiss on the cheek or holding hands. But for the majority of people, holding hands or even the simple touch of that other person's skin is too far. You may be thinking - you've got to be kidding! No. Touch is very powerful. Physical intimacy is meant to help bond and unite two people. One of the biggest lies ever told is, "Hey, that kiss (or any other intimate act) didn't mean anything!" If it doesn't mean anything, then why does it bring ties between two people?

I've heard so many people say we're "just friends"; "there really isn't anything romantic in our friendship"; "he's like my brother"; "she's like my sister," etc. But if two people spend too much time together, there can eventually be physical attraction there and the two will get into a bind that they didn't intend to happen. Once again, been there and done that too many times!

I had a guy friend where I was NOT at all attractive to him and we were, "BEST BUDS". We started being friends in a church group setting and we felt comfortable with each other. We didn't have to worry about either one of us liking the other. We even talked about our friendship and how we loved just being brother and sister in Christ. It so happened that one time there was a group of us at a restaurant and it was getting late. One by one everyone else went home and we sat there talking to each other for a long time because we became too comfortable with one another. We let our guards down.

Then out of nowhere, he touched my hand and something in me tingled and it felt good. The next thing I knew, we got in my car, found a dark parking lot and started making out. Even though I had no romantic feelings towards him, I didn't stay true to my convictions. So where did it go wrong? It all started with a simple touch from him. Instantly, my body reacted and I wanted more than just a touch. That one incident ruined our friendship for life.

Do you see how easily you can go down the wrong path with physical contact? Can you also see how easy it is to give into temptation when you are alone with someone? You should always have a group of people around you. If you find yourself alone with someone, immediately leave that situation. The longer you stay there, the tougher it will be to leave.

You have to know your weaknesses and set up boundaries BEFORE you get into a tempting situation. Once you get into that situation with no boundaries, you move quickly beyond the point of no return. When you are tempted (enticement to evil or sin), you must get as far away as you can! Why get into the boxing ring with a good chance of getting hit? Don't even step into it in the first place. How is this done? The answer is easy...RUN!

RUN means to get away as FAST as you can. Don't walk, linger or think about what you should do. Just run away from the situation. Don't look back! The longer you flirt with temptation, the harder it is to resist. You need to immediately detach yourself physically and emotionally.

FLEE from Sexual Immorality.
1 Corinthians 6:18

When you run away from the temptation,

where do you run to? JESUS! There is safety in Him if you remain under His care. Then pray for strength to be able to resist and stay away completely. Too many people see how far they can straddle the fence. It doesn't matter how much will-power you think you have. If you keep going to the edge to see how far you can go or look over, you will eventually fall... *GUARANTEED!*

I've had too many women tell me that they have detached themselves from the guy and have the situation under control. They are only saying "hi" and "bye" to each other, sending each other emails once in a while or talking on the phone "just for a couple of minutes to see how they are doing". They don't have it under control. It still has them under control because they still need to stay attached to that person in some little way.

Detachment is necessary once your boundaries have been broken. The best way to start over is by having NO CONTACT with that person for a period of time until you know for sure you are no longer emotionally attached. How will you know this? When you don't feel the urge to see that person, say hi or wonder how that person is doing. If any of this crosses your mind within at least a one-month period, then you are still attached.

Set boundaries and be UP FRONT with people. Lay it out for them. Ask them what types of boundaries they have in relationships. If they don't have any and think you are crazy, that is okay. God will honor you for standing firm in your convictions about boundaries. Plus that person knows from the start where you stand with relationships. Again, your accountability partner plays an important role with your boundaries. It can't be stressed enough how they can help you think straight when you feel tempted to throw your boundaries out the window.

Finally, write down your boundaries. Sometimes, when you get interested in someone, even if you have good intentions, you get a mental block. You need to write down ALL your boundaries and share them with your accountability partner before you get into a relationship or have an interest in someone. Also, think about various situations you might get into and how you would re-act to them. You can even take it as far as to role play with your accountability partner. Being prepared will help you make better decisions once you get into that type of situation. Writing it down will help you remember what your boundaries are. This will make it easier for you to stick to your convictions.

We don't live in a perfect world and sometimes we have to crash and burn before we learn. So, if you cross over a boundary, acknowledge it and confess it to God. Get on your knees, seek forgiveness and repentance. Then get back up and move forward. Look at your list of boundaries on a regular basis. Don't just write it down and stick it in a drawer somewhere. You need to have it where it is visible and you can access it on a regular basis, daily if necessary.

Time-Out #3

Boundaries I am setting for myself

Time:

1. _____
   _____

2. _____
   _____

3. _____
   _____

4. _____
   _____

5. _____
   _____

Emotions:

1. _____
   _____

2. _____

_____

3. _____

_____

4. _____

_____

5. _____

_____

Physical:

1. _____

_____

2. _____

_____

3. _____

_____

4. _____

_____

5. _____

_____

3

COMMITMENT

"Trusting God In Your Singleness"

Nowadays, commitment gets a bad rap among single adults. For instance, how often do you say you are going to do something or show up for something, and at the last minute cancel because you get a better offer or you just don't feel like going anymore? For many singles, this is common behavior, but as a Born-Again Virgin, you must be a person of your word. When you break your commitments, not only does it let people down but it also lets God down.

Make sure you intend to follow through before you make a commitment. It's better to say no than to leave someone hanging. It is easier to change a no to a yes, then a yes to a no. Commitment is a godly attribute to have.

Another C-word that gets a bad rap among singles is CELIBACY! For some of you, that is worse than the word "commitment". Let's take a look at both words. Commitment is an obligation to do something in the future. Celibacy is abstaining from sex. Both are choices that are made by Born-Again Virgins. Sometimes celibacy does not feel like a choice because no one is pursuing you. However, it is a choice because you can find someone to have sex with if you are desperate enough. I remember going to nightclubs to see if I could get lucky (and I usually did). For those of you that have had a promiscuous lifestyle, you know what I am talking about.

The Born-Again Virgin journey can be one of joy, wholeness and completeness. It doesn't have to be lonely, depressing and boring. Your commitment to God has to be a high priority. If you are committed to God, you will connect with him. He will show you how to live the abundant life the Bible talks about.

As a single person, you can be devoted to the Lord both in body and spirit. That means celibacy and commitment. Being celibate with your body and committing yourself spiritually to God during your season of singleness can be the best experience of your life.

I remember as a Christian single how intimate I was with God. Those were some of the best years of my life because I had so much alone time with God. I didn't have anyone else to take care of me every day. That made me trust God with everything in my life for he was my only source.

Married life comes with all kinds of obligations and responsibilities. So stop thinking the grass is greener on the other side because it's the same color whether you are married or single. The shade of green depends on how much you water and nurture your side of the fence.

An unmarried woman or virgin is concerned about the Lord's affairs; Her aim is to be devoted to the Lord in both body and spirit. But a married woman is concerned about the affairs of this world— how she can please her husband.
1 Corinthians 7:34

To feel fulfilled as a single and celibate adult, I had to make commitments to the Lord. The first one was making

Jesus my highest priority before anything or anyone else. Secondly, I chose to serve at the church which helped me stay connected to God and other believers. And last but not least, I had to start my day with prayer and praise. Making these commitments helped me not only with my season of singleness, but it helped me set priorities for the rest of my life. Now it's your turn to make your commitments unto the Lord.

 Time-Out #4

Commitments I am making to the Lord in my season of singleness:

1. _____

   _____

2. _____

   _____

3. _____

   _____

4. _____

_____

5. _____

_____

Let's step back and look at the word celibacy again. What is so good about being celibate? The Bible says you do well if you abstain from sexual immorality. You do well because it will not become a burden. Celibacy is important in order to live joyfully and contentedly on your journey as a Born-Again Virgin. Remember that you are committing your body to the Lord when you live a celibate lifestyle.

This is no easy task in today's culture. Magazines, television, billboards, the Internet, friends and even family members encourage promiscuity, pornography, lust, and affairs. But when you are a Born-Again Virgin, God loves you too much to let you take a path that leads you to pain and loss of dignity. Celibacy protects you not only physically, but emotionally, and spiritually. If you desire of keeping your purity, you must embrace celibacy until your wedding night.

Sanctification refers to being set apart from sin into holiness. In this context, it means being set apart from sexual impurity, in particular, holding oneself away from immorality by following the instructions in 1 Thessalonians 4:4-8. Born-Again Virgins are set-aside in purity and holiness.

> *It seemed good to the Holy Spirit and to us not to burden you with anything beyond the following requirements: You are to abstain from food sacrificed to idols, from blood, from the meat of strangled animals and from sexual immorality. You will do well to avoid these things*
> *Acts 15:28-29*

It's a lifestyle. Commitment and Celibacy are your friends! Don't be afraid of them. They will bring you protection and peace for your Born-Again Virgin journey.

> *It is God's will that you should be sanctified; that you should avoid sexual immorality; that each one of you should learn to control his own body in a way that is holy and honorable, not in passionate lust like the heathen, who do not know God*
> *1 Thessalonians 4:3-5*

4

X-RAY VISION

"Seeing Yourself Through God's Eyes"

Look with me of what an x-ray machine shows. Even though you may look fine on the outside, the x-ray machine can show hidden things like broken bones. God's x-ray vision shows things that are hidden inside of our hearts.

I can fool people by how I look on the outside but not God. He sees through my mask and straight to my heart. He sees when I have a deceitful or joyful heart. He can see inside where nobody else can. I cannot fool him for he is an all-seeing and all-knowing God.

> *From heaven the Lord looks down and sees all mankind; from his dwelling place he watches all who live on earth — he who forms the hearts of all who considers everything they do.*
> *Psalm 33:13-15*

It amazes me how I can know that God sees everything yet I still do things I know I shouldn't do. If I could only hear God audibly each time, he would be saying, "I saw that." Even though I know he sees, I act like he doesn't. I can imagine God shaking his head from side to side, with a smile on his face when I try to hide something from his x-ray vision.

The Bible says that God knew you before you were born because he is the Creator of everything. Yes,

For you created my inmost being; you knit me together in my mother's womb. I praise you because I am fearfully and wonderfully made.
Psalm 139:13-14

that means he created not only your body, but all the unique characteristics that make you – YOU. Some people are more outgoing and aggressive than others. Then there are those that are more introverted and quiet. This does not mean one type is better than the other. The body of Christ needs all types of people to balance each other out.

There are many personality tests to help you find out more about yourself. These self-examination tests put you into a category with other people that have similar characteristics. There are even tests that will tell you your personality type based on your body type. There was one test with results stating that if you are plump, you are social and fun. But if you are skinny, you are quiet and timid. I find this a bit silly because I know plenty of people that are plump that are quiet and I know skinny people that are pretty loud and obnoxious!

Don't get me wrong, these tests may be fun to take, but God did not create you as a personality type but as a person. God does not make carbon copies. He made you unique from everyone else in this world. Even twins have their own identity. Do you know who you are? Answer the following questions to find out how much you know about yourself.

Time-Out #5

1. WHO AM I? _____

_____

_____

2. WHO DOES GOD SAY THAT I AM? _____

_____

_____

3. WHAT AM I? _____

_____

_____

4. WHAT DOES GOD SAY THAT I AM? _____

_____

_____

5. HOW DO I VIEW MYSELF? _____

_____

_____

6. HOW DOES GOD VIEW ME? _____

_____

_____

You were born with certain characteristics like the color of our eyes. You have no control over these characteristics. Now, traits like integrity or generosity you will have to work to develop. This is especially difficult to maintain in today's corrupt society.

The most important character trait to have on this journey of life is integrity. Integrity is what you do when no one else is looking. For instance, do you only work hard when your boss is around? Do you ever "borrow" supplies from work to use at home? Even if you take a pen without telling your boss, you're stealing from your company. How about if you go to school and you come across a piece of paper with all the answers to a test you are going to take? Do you take it with you and cheat or do you rip it up and not look at it? Come on now! Only you know what you do behind closed doors. To succeed as a Born-Again Virgin, you must take integrity with you on the journey.

You determine which character traits you want to develop. Think of it like a salad bar where you choose the type of lettuce, variety of toppings, even the salad dressing. You choose what goes on the plate. It's the same concept with character traits. You choose which one you want to have in your life. The smorgasbords of godly traits are love, loyalty, truthfulness, contentment, dependability…just to name a few. If you are not portraying these godly traits, then you are choosing to develop negative traits like hatred, procrastination, unreliable, lying, etc.

Whether you like it or not, you will be judged by your character. It doesn't matter how gifted or talented you think you are. That will only get you so far in life. Remember that anyone can make it to the top, but it is your character that will keep you there.

When you accept Jesus into your life, you become a child of God. God says you are his child

> *Yet to all who received Him, to those who believed in His name, He gave the right to become children of God- Children born not of natural descent, nor of human decision or a husband's will, but born of God.*
> *John 1:12-13*

and you need to see that about yourself! Being a child of God has benefits. When you fully understand that you are a child of God, you get to share in his treasures and promises. You get to walk in freedom, live a pure life, and receive spiritual wisdom that is reserved only for the children of God.

God's x-ray vision sees you as a unique and perfect person in his eyes. Since God made you unique and special to this world, it is an insult to him when you want to be somebody else like a supermodel, movie star or a famous athlete. Only you can be what God wants you to be. Nobody can be you and you cannot be somebody else.

You are one of a kind. You are perfect in his eyes. How can this be, you ask? Because the Bible says so! You cannot be perfect on your own, but when you are in Christ and he is in you, he sees you as perfect. It may be hard to comprehend this,

Be perfect, therefore, as your heavenly Father is perfect.
Matthew 5:48

but the Holy Spirit will show you how God sees you through his x-ray vision. All you have to do is ask!

5

YOUR THOUGHTS

"What's On Your Mind"

Most of my problems begin with my thought life. Gaining control over my old way of thinking has been a challenge. Daily, I see the need of renewing my mind. Because I came from a worldly background prior to being born-again, I had to learn some new ways of thinking. I turned to the Bible as my roadmap for life and the only source for renewing my mind.

> *Do not conform any longer to the pattern of this world, but be transformed by the renewing of your mind. Then you will be able to test and approve what God's will is – His good, pleasing and perfect will.*
> *Romans 12:2*

I learned God's will by replacing my human way of thinking with God's way of thinking. I learned through reading the Bible how to be more sensitive to the Holy Spirit. Sometimes, I felt something inside of me saying, "That is not a good idea in this situation." That is called conviction. I had to learn to listen and be obedient to this.

When a little child is about to hurt itself, a good parent will say, "Don't do that", to warn the child of danger. However, it is up to the child to decide on what to do. That child can either obey the parent and not get hurt or disobey and continue to do what is going to get them hurt. In the same way, God will warn you before you get into a relationship.

There are warnings throughout the Bible. God sent people to warn others and even spoke to individuals directly. Warnings were always followed by consequences. Some were good and some were bad depending on how people responded. God will warn you when you are headed down the wrong path. It's up to you whether you listen or not.

> *You were taught, with regard to your former way of life, to put off your old self, which is being corrupted by its deceitful desires; to be made new in the attitude of your minds; and to put on the new self, created to be like God in true righteousness and holiness.*
> *Ephesians 4:22-24*

According to Ephesians 4:22-24, a Born-Again Virgin must approach life with a Christ-like attitude. It starts with the way Jesus would think. What would Jesus think when you are interested in someone? Would he lust after that person the way you used to when you were in the world? Or would he think highly of that person and respect that person. To have a Christ-like attitude, you need to continually ask how Jesus would think in every situation. You need to have true righteousness and holiness in your thought life. The only one that can help you is Jesus.

 Time-Out #6

What are some *"THOUGHTS"* that come to mind when you think of a relationship?

_____

_____

_____

_____

_____

Even the most level-headed person can get stuck on stupid when an attractive person shows an interest. Wisdom, logic, and common sense all go out the window. I've seen it happen time and time again when I meet someone attractive. I don't think straight. I can't eat. I daydream ALL DAY long. When people are talking to me, I don't really listen to them. I hear them, but don't listen because my mind is with that guy I am interested in. I write my first name with HIS LAST NAME to see how I would sign my full name.

Sometimes even before I've actually met the guy, just on looks alone, within seconds, we are married, have 2.5 kids, a home with a white picket fence, a dog named Rover and are living happily ever after. Has this ever happened to you? Here I am in my thirties acting like I am in high school again.

So, let's take a look at how it starts with just a thought. A thought as simple as "he's cute" can turn into "I'm cute too"; "we both would be cute together"; and if we had kids we would have "cute kids", "live in a cute house", and so on and so on. Do you see how easy *"A THOUGHT"* can turn into more?

The Bible states in **Psalms 94:11 - The Lord knows the thoughts of man, he knows that they are futile.** When you daydream and let your imagination run wild, it is futile to God. What does futile mean? It means serving no useful purpose, completely ineffective. I can honestly say that when I daydream about someone, it is meaningless. Nothing ever comes of it except heartaches and disappointments. It's a make-believe fairy tale in my own mind. It's a false expectation that is far from reality that does not please God at all. This could lead to an unhealthy thought life which could result in unhealthy relationships.

In Romans 8:6-8, enmity means enemy or evil against God. When you use your natural human way of thinking, you are doing evil against God. You cannot PLEASE God when your thoughts are not spiritually minded. You may even hear Christians say that it's not sin as long as you don't do it. But that is

For to be carnally minded is death; but to be spiritually minded is life and peace. Because the carnal mind is enmity against God: for it is not subject to the law of God, neither indeed can be. So then they that are in the flesh cannot please God.
Romans 8:6-8 (KJV)

not what the Bible says. In **Matthew 5:27-28, Jesus teaches, "You have heard that it was said, 'Do not commit adultery.' But I tell you that anyone who looks at a woman lustfully has already committed adultery with her in his heart."**

I used to think that my thought life was all innocence – a Cinderella Fairly Tale. I realized I was kidding myself when these thoughts came up while I was in church trying to worship God. As I was singing a worship song, an image of a guy I was interested popped up into my mind. The next thing I knew, I was visualizing this guy naked while I was singing about God's holiness. I have to be especially careful about my thought life because I was sexually active before becoming a Christian.

My so-called innocent thoughts can quickly turn into lustful ones. Lust refers to those thoughts that focus on

"What comes out of a man is what makes him 'unclean.' For from within, out of men's hearts, come evil thoughts, sexual immorality, theft, murder, adultery, greed, malice, deceit, lewdness, envy, slander, arrogance and folly. All these evils come from inside and make a man 'unclean.'"
Mark 7:20-23

getting pleasure from sexual satisfaction. This doesn't necessarily have to be thoughts of intercourse, but the romance of someone sweeping you off your feet to wine and dine you, like the scenes from a Hollywood movie.

Let's take a deeper look at how your senses affect your thought life. Sight, touch, smell, taste and hearing are all windows to your soul affecting how you think. What you see will feed into your thoughts. Look at all the sensuality on TV and movies today that creeps in to your thoughts and maybe even your behavior. How often do you see a fast food commercial and then run out and get that burger and fries because you saw it in the commercial?

Visuals are very influential and will have a long-term effect on your thought life. The eyes are the gateway to the body, soul and spirit. Whatever you allow in through your eyes will fill your entire being. So, if you look at pornography, you will fill your mind with porn images. It's the same with violent movies or even video games. Your mind will be full of violence.

There was a season in my life I had to fast movies. This was not just rated R but also rated PG-13, particularly those cute, supposedly innocent, romantic movies. Some of those PG-13 movies could still get me hot and bothered and all worked up.

Watching these romantic movies made me live in a fantasy. I would see myself living in the body of that person and falling in love with that perfect man on the movie screen. Then what happened when I was done watching that movie? I would have this big urge to have a relationship and desire to have sex. My mind was consumed with what I saw on the screen. So I stayed away from romantic movies until I was strong enough in my spiritual walk that it didn't affect my thought life anymore.

No one lights a lamp and puts it in a place where it will be hidden, or under a bowl. . Instead he puts it on its stand, so that those who come in may see the light. Your eye is the lamp of your body. When your eyes are good, your whole body also is full of light. But when they are bad, your body also is full of darkness. See to it, then, that the light within you is not darkness. Therefore, if your whole body is full of light, and no part of it dark, it will be completely lighted, as when the light of a lamp shines on you.
Luke 11:33-36

We have a responsibility as Christians to ensure that we are not feeding our eyes with evil. If we choose to look at wholesome and good things, we will be full of light, shining like a lamp. If we choose bad things, then we are full of darkness and evil.

Let's look at the sense of touch. What happens when someone brushes up against you and touches you? Your body re-acts whether it's good or bad. When a mother holds her baby, her touch is nurturing and pleasant. This is a good reaction to touch.

Touch can get you in trouble when you are interested in someone. This sense can make your whole body tingle, from the top of your head to the soles of your feet. When this happens, you will desire more than that initial touch. This can lead into making out, petting, oral sex and eventually intercourse. Wow, all that from one simple touch!

Next, let's look at the sense of smell. Ever smell someone with cologne on? Does that do something to you, like drive you crazy? I love men that wear cologne. However, certain colognes bring back memories of certain relationships. Every time I had a new boyfriend, I would buy him a new cologne scent. This was to make sure he had a type of cologne that didn't bring back memories of old boyfriends.

How about the sense of taste? When you have a taste of an alcoholic drink, does it make you want to get loose and friendly with someone? The taste of an alcoholic drink can connect you to the way you used to be in bars and night clubs. The craving may get you to the point of drinking heavily again or doing things that you used to do when intoxicated.

Take a look at the sense of hearing. Think about what you're listening to. Music is "Mood". It affects the soul, specifically stirring up emotions. This in turn will manipulate your brain. Music can bring you up when you're down, and vice-versa. It will bring you down and relax you when you are hyper or have anxiety. That is what music did to Saul whenever he had an evil spirit on him. He brought David to play the harp to calm and relax him.

You get caught up with your feelings when you listen to music. It can take you to a different dimension. Music also has a big influence in society.

Fashion statements come from music videos. Certain attitudes and actions are related to certain kinds of music. Sex, drugs and alcohol are becoming normal in society through music. Music influences the younger generation in a powerful way. The more you listen to worldly music that sings about sexuality, violence or anything else that is not edifying, you will subconsciously start thinking about this and then doing the things that the lyrics describe.

All secular music is not bad for you. The lyric is what makes secular music bad, because lyrics get imbedded within your soul. How often do you hear a song that you haven't heard for many, many years, and you still remember every single word like you just heard it yesterday? Yet, you can't remember what you read in the Bible last week.

I thought listening to worldly love songs was okay. After all, it didn't have any violence or sensuality to the words. However, when I heard a love song, I wanted to be in a relationship. It made me long to be with someone just by listening to music about love. Certain songs take me back to my old lifestyle. It would remind me of old boyfriends and I would feel the urge to call them just to see how they are doing. If I did that, it would re-open the door to my past. There is danger in listening to the same music you listened to from your past. This can drag you away and entice you to go back to your old life style.

All of your senses will feed into your thoughts, whether it's good or bad. If you allow certain movies, TV shows, music or internet sites to influence your thought life, you will be more vulnerable to lust. As a Christian, this will be an on-going, daily battle as long as you live on this earth. Every battle that you are fighting has to be conquered in the mind, first.

For though we live in the world, we do not wage war as the world does. The weapons we fight with are not the weapons of the world. On the contrary, they have divine power to demolish strongholds. We demolish arguments and every pretension that sets itself up against the knowledge of God, and we take captive every thought to make it obedient to Christ. And we will be ready to punish every act of disobedience, once your obedience is complete.
2 Corinthians 10:3-6

Every thought must be taken captive and made obedient to

God's word. For example, if you start thinking about dating a guy or marrying him, STOP and ask yourself, "Is this pleasing to God and does this glorify God?" Be truthful with yourself. If you cannot answer yes to this, then you must immediately stop thinking about it and fill your mind with scriptures. What did Jesus do when he was tempted? **He answered back with, "It is written" (Luke 4:1-14).**

Jesus is the example you must follow. Filling your mind with scriptures and good thoughts will help you overcome temptation. So when you are tempted, you can say "It is written" *(a verse in the Bible dealing with that temptation).* If you don't learn to do this, these so-called innocent thoughts will turn into sinful actions.

For the word of God is living and active. Sharper than any double-edged sword, it penetrates even to dividing soul and spirit, joints and marrow; it judges the thoughts and attitudes of the heart. Nothing in all creation is hidden from God's sight. Everything is uncovered and laid bare before the eyes of him to whom we must give account.
Hebrews 4:12-13

Each time the thought comes back up, continue to use scripture to fight it. Don't beat yourself up if it keeps coming back. It may come back 50 times in one day, 49 times the next day, and 45 times the following day. That is okay for there is no condemnation to those who are in Christ Jesus. You just have to keep trying and pushing through each unpleasant thought that comes up. This will teach you discipline which will turn into self-control, one of the characteristics of the fruit of the spirit.

The word of God is the most powerful tool to overcome your thought life. Keep repeating scriptures over and over again until that bad thought eventually leaves your mind. As you exercise this every day, it will get easier and before you know it, these thoughts won't come back as often or not at all.

 Time-Out #7

Philippians 4:8, 9: Finally Brethren, whatever is true, whatever is noble, whatever is right, whatever is pure, whatever is lovely, whatever is admirable, if anything is excellent or praiseworthy, think about such things.

What are some **"whatever"** things to think about?

True (fact/reality): _____

_____

_____

_____

Noble (possessing outstanding qualities): _____

_____

_____

_____

Right (righteous/upright): _____

_____

_____

_____

Pure (free from harshness/roughness, spotless): _____

_____

_____

_____

Lovely (lovable): _____

_____

_____

_____

Admirable (deserving the highest esteem): _____

_____

_____

_____

Excellent: (Superior, Praiseworthy, to glorify):_____

_____

_____

_____

Conquering your thought life doesn't happen overnight. It's a process called transformation. Maybe you were promiscuous when you were in the world. That process happened over time. Being transformed into the godly single adult God is calling you to be will take time as well.

Song of Solomon is romantic and a sexual story but it warns you, "Do not awaken love before it's time". When you start thinking about relationships, you might feel sexual desires. It may not necessary lead to sexual intercourse with someone, but it can lead to masturbation, pornography, cyber-sex, etc.

Once you take one of these paths, you will find yourself wanting more and more until eventually you are having intercourse or doing other immoral things without any remorse. But if you obey God's word by NOT AWAKENING love before it's time, he will bring blessings beyond measure even in the area of sexual fulfillment when you do it the right way. This must start with your thought life!

Vilma Conner

6

ZEALOUS ATTITUDE

"Attitude Adjustment"

Attitude is half the battle. You might be tempted to join the band-wagon with critical people in your family, at work, or even on TV but negativity will latch onto you and spread throughout your soul. But as a Born-Again Virgin, you must have a zealous attitude, eagerly pursuing Jesus. If you are positive about your journey, you will enjoy it more.

Having a zealous attitude was difficult for me because some of my friends were critical of my singleness. Even family member's critical comments started affecting my spirit. I started carrying a negative

Your attitude should be the same as that of Christ Jesus.
Philippians 2:5

attitude and judging others. I loved my family and friends, but they were bringing me down. I found that the more I hung around them, the more I started becoming negative about everything. I felt like I had this black cloud following me around, keeping me down in the dumps. I couldn't stand myself until I got a revelation from God of how to make an attitude adjustment.

The first change I made was to accept the fact that God was with me in the season of singleness. He didn't want me to be anxious about anything, including wanting to be married. I could enjoy being single or I could be miserable. It was my choice. Since I couldn't change my circumstances, I chose to accept them which made me feel happier.

> Do not be anxious about anything, but in everything, by prayer and petition, with thanksgiving, present your requests to God. And the peace of God, which transcends all understanding, will guard your hearts and your minds in Christ Jesus.
> Philippians 4:6, 7

The second change I made was to surround myself with positive people. There are millions of

Christians in this world. So, I chose to surround myself with Christians who brought joy into my life. I learned to stay away from those people who were negative about being single.

The third change I made was to show an attitude of gratitude. Being thankful should not only be at Thanksgiving time. I needed to get into a habit of being thankful on a daily basis. Thankfulness gives me a positive attitude no matter what life throws at me. Now, I thank God even for little

Be joyful always; pray continually; give thanks in all circumstances, for this is the will for you in Christ Jesus. 1 Thessalonians 5:16-18

things such as a roof over my head, food on the table and clothes on my back. I realized I have more than enough when I took a look in my closet and counted the pairs of shoes I have!

Adjusting your attitude for the journey is vital in having the zeal you need to survive as a Born-Again Virgin. If you don't, this can slow you down on your journey. Or worse, it can take you on a long detour of negativism. Look at what happened to the Israelites being in the wilderness for all those years. And because of their attitudes, they never saw the Promise Land. Take a zealous attitude with you on the journey. If you do, God will give you the joy about being single throughout your journey.

 ## *Time-Out #8*

What are some things you are anxious or restless about?

_____

_____

_____

_____

Who are some positive people that you surround yourself with?

_____

_____

_____

_____

What are some things to be thankful for?

_____

_____

_____

_____

Conclusion:

These basics tools will become part of your survival kit to help you on the journey. Once you have your picked your Accountability partners, Boundaries are defined, Commitments are made, X-ray vision is set, Your thought life under control and a Zealous attitude in place, the Holy Spirit can guide you. He will give you revelations in your singleness and in the area of relationships.

The Word of God will uphold you in times of temptation. Your accountability partners will help you stay on the right track when you cannot do it on your own. Remember you will continue to learn new things about being a Born-Again Virgin, no matter how young or old you are. Just sit back and enjoy this journey as you have just learned the basics!

Vilma Conner

PART II

Recess Break

7

SABBATICAL

"Taking Time Off"

One of the smartest things you can do is take a break from romantic relationships. Why? This helps you re-focus your life and get back to the important things God has for you. Some relationships will distract you from the path God wants you on. Distractions can delay that special relationship God has for you.

When people come to me because they don't know how to handle distractions, I tell them to take a break, or "Sabbatical". A sabbatical is a change from a normal routine. Can I suggest a sabbatical year? This means a year of rest from dating and relationships. You may be thinking, "No way Jose! That is a long time!" Is it really? What is one year compared to the rest of your life? Look at the book of **Esther** in the Bible. Read her story if you are not familiar with it. She took one year to prepare to be a queen. That is a small sacrifice for what she became for the rest of her life. Do you want to be the best person you can be for your mate when you get married? Well, you need to take a time-out for yourself in preparing spiritually, physically, and emotionally.

Before I became a Christian, I always had a boyfriend. If I knew a guy was ready to break up with me, I made sure I had someone else ready for back up. I found my identity in men. When I became born-again, I had a mature Christian friend challenge me to go on a sabbatical with her for one month. She said it would be good for us to take a break from guys and to spend more time with God. I thought it was a bit weird, but I took the challenge.

We decided not to date anyone during this one-month period. This included one-on-one time with a guy or talking on the phone with a guy. We kept each other accountable. If it wasn't for the accountability, I couldn't have done this on my own.

Do you know how many guys flocked towards us during this one-month period? It was like all the guys came out of the wood-work and started asking us out. However, we kept our vows not only to each other but to God, our Father. We did not want to disappoint him. The Bible says, let our "Yes" be "Yes" and our "No" be "No".

After that month, we extended our sabbatical to three months, then to six months. At six months, my friend decided she was ready to date. However, God had not released me yet and I made a commitment to do it for a full year. I learned so much about myself within that year. God showed me things that I never noticed before because there was always a guy distracting me. Since I was faithful to God within the sabbatical year, I finally learned to have my identity in Christ rather than in men or relationships. God showed me how to have a real relationship with him and him alone.

I felt like Esther spending a whole year in preparation for my greatest love, Jesus, and for the first time in my life, I was okay with being single. Even though I sometimes felt lonely, I realized I was never alone, because Jesus was always there by my side. Jesus became so real to me during this sabbatical.

Taking a sabbatical from dating is a way to acknowledge Jesus in your daily walk of life. I'm not saying that you have to isolate yourself from the world. What I am saying is that you need to keep your distance from the opposite sex for awhile so that you will not be distracted by temptation.

First and foremost, you need to have mentors in your life. Esther's mentor was Mordecai. He knew that Esther had a chance of a future like no other, so he guided her in what to say and what not to say while she was in her preparation time. In the same way, you need to find mentors that are godly people who love Jesus with all of their heart. Make sure they know the word of God for guidance and protection. This mentor should know what it means to be a child of our Father in heaven. It will help you make your heavenly Father the highest priority in life.

A mentor is different than an accountability partner. A mentor is someone you look up to as a good example of how to live a godly life. The Bible states, in

Titus 2:4, that "Older women are to train the younger women." Ladies, you can learn a lot from older women because they have life experience. Some of you might think older women aren't up to date with the culture, but wisdom is not about the greatest and latest fashion trend; it's about making good decisions throughout life. Think of it this way, if you listen to older women's advice, you might learn from their mistakes so that you don't make so many of your own.

It is important that you prepare yourself spiritually. I've heard guys say time and time again that they are looking for a godly woman. They admire the way women pray, worship and spend time with God through reading the word, church activities and how they treat others. Guys are observant in this area. Ladies, you never know when a guy is watching you from a distance.

There is nothing more attractive to guys than a woman who is beautiful not only on the outside, but most importantly on the inside. Guys can tell when a woman is truly in love with Jesus. It is a character trait that godly men look for in a wife. The secret to successful preparation is to change from the inside out. It starts within the heart which will overflow to your outward appearance.

The next person that mentored Esther was Hegai. He was in charge of all the ladies and taught them how to act like royalty. She found favor with him, so he provided a special place for her, beauty treatments and special food. Did you hear that? She had beauty treatments. Yes, this meant physical beauty treatments. She also had special food which meant it's not what everyone else ate. Sounds like a diet to me.

You must learn to take care of your physical being. Some people may think that this is vain, but if Esther did this in the Bible, you can follow that example. Let's face it, ladies, men are visual and they are attracted to how we look. I can get an "Amen" from the fellas about this. Looking like something the cat dragged in is not going to be attractive to anybody. If you want to live like royalty, you have to start looking like it. I'm not saying you have to look your best everyday or spend a lot of money, but it is okay to spend some time on your hair before you go out in public.

I have many single female friends that are too lazy to get fixed up a little. They claim they have the "natural" look. However, I have seen them when they do get fixed up and how men notice them. Looking good on the outside will not hurt anyone. We need to take care of our physical bodies, even if it means waking up 30 minutes earlier in the morning. In **1 Timothy 2:9**, it states that women should be modest in their appearance. Ladies, this means to look decent, don't go over-board or under-board.

Now let's talk about those comfortable sweats that you love to wear around the house. You know, the ones that you've have had for years. They have holes, stains and the material is faded because it's been washed over a thousand times already. They are so comfortable that you don't want to get rid of them. Don't get rid of them, but please don't go out in public in them.

Imagine putting on sweatpants, a wrinkled blouse, high heeled shoes, and heading to the store.

Everything is mismatched and looks like you just rolled out of bed. Do you expect a guy to be attracted to you looking this way? A guy may look at you, but not because he is attracted to you. That double take is probably because he thinks you had one rough night.

Your natural body scent is another thing to think about. This will not get you far. There is nothing worse than hanging out with a group of people and someone has body odor. And guess what? It happens to be you. Use some deodorant and perfume to cover up your funk. If there is still a funky smell, then check your clothes especially if it's something that you have already worn a few times this past week. Smell the underarms of that shirt and the crotch area of those pants. Here's a hint: if there is an odor, even a slight odor, don't wear it! Personal hygiene is imperative.

Now let's talk about the other end of the spectrum of going over-board. This is when you are so concerned about looking superb that you cannot relax and let your hair down. I remember going on a short-term mission trip with my single's group. There were a group of ladies that would wake up hours earlier than everyone else to make sure their hair and make-up was on perfectly before anyone saw them. Talk about high maintenance. This was a mission trip not a vacation.

We were literally in the ditches digging dirt to help build an orphanage. By the end of the day, those ladies looked like the rest of us no matter how much make-up they wore. And their clothes were just as filthy as everyone else's. Don't get caught up with outward appearance. It is all about finding the right balance in your physical appearance.

Lastly, you have to learn the right balance in expressing your emotions. The biggest mistake a woman can make is to think that she can get her emotional needs met by men. They don't have a clue nor should you expect them to. God made men and women different. Don't put so much pressure on men with your emotions. They have enough to worry about in a relationship. Women should share their emotions with each other and not so much with the opposite sex.

Let's take a look at Esther again. She was assigned maids during her year of preparation. When you spend a lot of time with people, even if they are under you, you become friends with them. Her maids where there to support her emotionally and were good accountability to help her to stay out of trouble.

If you feel you have deep emotional wounds, get some counseling to help you deal with your issues. Dumping your pain on others will put a strain on all your relationships especially romantic ones. No one wants to put up with an emotional basket case. Find a Christian counselor that can direct you with Biblical truths in dealing with your issues. If you go to the secular world for counseling, it might not line up with the word of God. Only with the help of God, the Holy Spirit and the word of God, can you truly be spiritually and emotionally set free from emotional bondage. This is all part of the journey of being a Born-Again Virgin that God has called you to for such a time as this!

Time-Out #9

1. Am I ready to prepare myself for my mate?

   Yes   No   Not Yet

2. If yes: I will start my one year sabbatical on: _____
   (don't wait, start today!)

   If no: why I am not ready:_____

   _____

   _____

   If not yet: when will I be:_____

   _____

   _____

3. Stop and say a prayer right now regarding this preparation
   time. Ask God to show you how to prepare yourself the way
   Esther prepared herself.

4. List ways that God is calling you to prepare yourself:

PHYSICAL:

☐ _____

☐ _____

☐ _____

☐ _____

EMOTIONAL:

☐ _____

☐ _____

☐ _____

☐ _____

SPIRITUAL:

☐ _____

_____

☐ _____

_____

☐ _____

_____

☐ _____

_____

FINANCES:

☐ _____

_____

☐ _____

_____

☐ _____

_____

☐ _____

_____

Vilma Conner

8

DWELL IN IT OR
DEAL WITH IT

"Evaluating Past Relationships"

As you continue on the Born-Again Virgin journey, you must get rid of old baggage that is weighing you down! Could it be the baggage of un-forgiveness or possibly bitterness? Most of the baggage you carry throughout life comes from relationships.

You might be carrying heavy baggage from a past relationship without realizing it. You know you are miserable about something but don't know why. Situations may arise and you are bothered in your spirit but cannot pinpoint what is causing it.

Picture yourself having a heavy backpack that is slowing you down from hiking up a mountain. You stop to look inside to see why it is so heavy. Once you open your backpack, you notice there are rocks inside. It is common sense to remove these rocks so they won't be a burden to you while trying to hike up the mountain, right?

Let's go back in time and evaluate the types of heavy rocks that could be weighing you down. Relationships you have had in the past must be re-visited. I'm not saying you have to dig up your past or even worse, dwell in it. What I am saying is that you must go back in time to find patterns of destructive behaviors in relationships that may be keeping you from being healthy in current or future relationships.

How do you know where you are going if you don't first stop and see where you have been? Stop going around that same mountain! Sometimes you don't even know that you are following the same pattern in choosing the wrong person over and over again. It is easier to see the mistakes that you have made, by evaluating where you have been. Then you can change it in your present before stepping into the future.

After evaluating relationships in my life, I noticed I was always in the same type of relationship. Even though it was a different guy, there was something familiar each time I was involved with someone. How did I come to this revelation? I'm so glad you asked. I had to experience this the hard way.

There was a period in my journey where I thought I was standing firm as a strong Christian single, but boy was I wrong! It started when I noticed a new guy in my single's group at church. He was a new believer and we started hanging out. There were red flags that went up inside

> So, if you think you are standing firm, be careful that you don't fall! No temptation has seized you except what is common to man. And God is faithful; He will not let you be tempted beyond what you can bear. But when you are tempted, He will also provide a way out so that you can stand up under it.
> 1 Corinthians 10:12-13

me but I thought I was strong enough and had everything under control. After all, I had been born-again for five years and had not dated anyone. Surely, I was mature and strong enough to stand this type of temptation.

This is the most dangerous place to be if there are no safeguards in place and you just rely on your own strength. As 1 Corinthians 10:12-13 states, God will provide a way out. It's up to you whether you take that escape or not.

Even though I knew better, I gave into temptation. The guy who was a new believer also confessed that he felt what we were doing was wrong. I agreed, but in my mind I said, "Oh but this is so enjoyable! I've been good for five years and a little fun won't hurt. Plus, I know how far to go and when to stop." Although conviction came over me, I chose to ignore the Holy Spirit. The Holy Spirit is a gentlemen and he will not force us into something we don't want to do.

Even after standing strong for many years, I fell back into my worldly ways. That season of my life was the craziest and most painful time on my journey. It was a hard lesson to learn. What started out as a friendship quickly became a sexual relationship and it was hard to stop. Remember those boundaries I talked about in Chapter 2? Once I stepped over the line, I was on the way to self-destruction.

When you are a Born-Again Virgin and you fall hard, you will either get back up again and move forward or fall completely away from the Lord. If you allow your flesh to rule your spirit, you will be tempted to leave your faith and go back to your old lifestyle. But, if you allow your spirit to rule your flesh, you will be able to move forward in your life. If you find yourself in the predicament of falling into sexual temptation, remember only Jesus can restore your purity. But you must put your hope in him again.

When I was in this relationship, I knew it was wrong. I did not feel the presence of God and that was the scariest and loneliest feeling in my life. I knew I needed to get right with God or I was surely going to destroy the rest of my life. When you have tasted the goodness of the Lord and have had that experience of closeness and intimacy with God, nothing can compare to it. I felt like the most horrible person on earth. I knew I had hurt God and I was very sorry for it. I had to repent. The key to coming back to the Lord is to come to him with a heart of repentance.

I felt led to take a self-retreat for a weekend. I stayed in a hotel on the beach by myself, something I had never done before. I fasted, prayed and just had me and God time. There were no distractions, no TV, no internet, no friends, no family, etc. The Holy Spirit led me to make a list of all my past relationships and start journaling about them. I realized I still had a lot of baggage from my past that was weighing me down. Some relationships were hard to think about as I still had a lot of hurts and disappointments from them. My relationship with my stepfather and the lack of relationship with my biological father were both tough to honestly look at.

After I journal about the positive and negative effects from relationships with friends and family, the Holy Spirit let me to examine my sexual relationships. This was the toughest list to do as it brought up a lot of emotions that I thought were gone. It felt like this monster inside of me wanting to come out – an angry, hateful monster that wanted revenge! The Holy Spirit gently pointed out to me that there was still some unforgiveness in my heart.

Unforgiveness is poison to your spirit. If you hold anger or bitterness towards someone, you will be chained to your past. This allows that person to continue to hurt you in your present life and will affect your future. If you have unforgiveness towards people, you must forgive them because in **Matthew 6:14, Jesus says, " For if you forgive men when they sin against you, your heavenly Father will also forgive you, but if you don't forgive men their sins, your Father will not forgive your sins."**

Forgiveness is a choice. Forgiveness is letting go of that hurt or pain caused by someone else. This does not mean you are letting that person get away with what they did to you. You have no control over that. What you are doing is releasing yourself from the hurt that came from the situation with the person. You are deciding that it is not going to affect you anymore. You will experience FREEDOM for yourself when you forgive someone. Make a decision right now to forgive anyone on your list who has hurt you.

The following is a sample forgiveness prayer:

Dear heavenly Father,

Thank you for forgiving me of all my sins.

Now, I choose to forgive [name the person]

for [what he or she did to me] because it made me

feel [list emotions like angry, rejected, shameful, dirty,

worthless, etc.] Jesus, I receive the freedom of forgiveness

and ask you help to me walk in this freedom for the

rest of my life. Amen.

Now back to the story of my self-retreat. I took each relationship on my list and started writing what I felt about each one. I remembered each man and all the emotions that had been bottled up inside for years. All the hurts and disappointments came to the surface and I knew I had to deal with it once and for all!

I started with my biological father since he was the first man in my life. As I wrote about him, the Holy Spirit showed me how the hurt started with abandonment and rejection. I was shocked by this revelation because I never knew my biological father yet he still had some effect on my life as a child and even as an adult.

The next important man in my life was my stepfather. He disappointed me in the areas of trust, love and protection. I felt I didn't receive this from the only father figure in my childhood. Innocent affection turned into inappropriate behavior between a father and a daughter. Being molested left me with anger, bitterness and hatred towards my stepfather and all the men following him in my life.

Looking back at these two earthly fathers who were not at all what they were supposed to be made me even more thankful for my Heavenly Father. I do have to say that God can bring reconciliation to broken relationships, if you let him. It took nearly twenty years for my stepfather and me to reconcile our relationship as father and daughter. It was hard to talk about it, but God

> *"I will be a Father to you, and you will be my sons and daughters", says the Lord almighty*
> *2 Corinthians 6:18*

changed our broken hearts to mended ones. Now we have that father - daughter relationship that I always wanted in my life.

I want to take a moment to talk about our Heavenly Father. I hear countless of women that I counsel say they don't know what it's like to have a relationship with God as a Father. They know Jesus, but have a difficult time with seeing God as a Father. I was the same way. I had a great relationship with Jesus and can relate to him being my friend, buddy, lover, brother, etc. But when it came to God as a Father, it was hard to comprehend it.

I really believe it is because you relate to God the way you relate to your earthly father. Now, having bad father figures in your life, it distorts what your Heavenly Father is really like. But understand this; he will never treat you bad. He is the Father of love and that is what he wants to shower you with. His love will never be compared to anyone or anything else in your life.

I remember talking to Jesus about this during prayer one morning. I said, "Jesus, I know how to have a relationship with you, but I don't know how to have one with Father God. Your word says in John 14:6 that you are the way, the truth and the life. No one comes to the Father except through you. Please show me how to have this relationship with God the Father through you who already have that relationship with him." It was that simple.

See, Jesus is the bridge that takes us to God himself. Within minutes of this prayer, I had this overwhelming experience come over me! It was as if God came from behind me and gave me the biggest spiritual bear hug! It was the most sensational feeling and the start of my relationship with my Daddy – Abba Father! I felt like that little girl in daddy's arms that I have craved for all my life.

Now, let's get back to my journaling. I also wrote about my brothers. They were important males during my childhood. I can say those were probably the only normal relationships I had with the opposite sex. It's funny that I can look back now and say we had healthy relationships. Although growing up, I hated them and they got on my nerves. Anyone have siblings like this? Now my brothers and I can look back and have a good laugh at our sibling rivalries.

Once I finished journaling about all the males in my family, I made a list of two categories of relationships I had with guys. The first was a list of all the guys I had sexual intercourse with. The second were guys I did not have sex with. The first out-numbered the second, which I found astonishing. I was also a bit embarrassed at myself for having one-night stands and forgetting the names of the guys. So I wrote John Doe #1, John Doe #2, etc. Although I was embarrassed, I knew being real with God was the only way to go.

Listing all the good and bad qualities in each person and the relationship took a whole weekend. Once I evaluated each guy and the relationship, I had to assess myself in these relationships. I wrote down all my feelings, particularly any hurts I had toward each guy. I also wrote the reason for the breakup and any lessons that I learned. Seeing it all in writing was an important part in the process of evaluating all my relationships.

Time-Out #10

Sexual Relationships Evaluation

1. Name of Sexual Partner: _____

2. Length of time together: _____

3. Good Qualities in this person:_____

    _____

4. Bad Qualities in this person: _____

    _____

5. Good Memories about this relationship: _____

    _____

6. Bad Memories about this relationship: _____

    _____

7. My good feelings toward this person: _____

    _____

8. My bad feelings toward this person: _____

    _____

9. Reason for Breakup: _____

_____

10. Lesson Learned from this relationship: _____

_____

Find Evaluations on the website below:

 Internet Interactive Website: www.bavirgin.com
Book Entry Keyword: EVALUATIONS

The purpose of doing this is to identify patterns and behaviors of the past. The Holy Spirit revealed patterns of bad behavior and choices I made in men. Something that I did not realize I had until I saw it on paper. He showed me how I was in bondage – still chained to habits that were self-defeating.

The majority of the guys had patterns of being non-committal womanizers, and always needing excitement in their lives. As I prayed about these patterns, I realized that I was this way too. Usually what we don't like in other people is a mirror of what we need to work on ourselves.

Even though I dreamed of being married and committed, I was also afraid of commitment. I was attracted to guys I knew couldn't make the commitment either. I needed lots of men who made things exciting in my life. So, I would seek out guys who enjoyed the excitement of being a womanizer. It was a challenge for me to go after guys that everyone else wanted. It was as though I had won the prize over the rest of the competition. I, in turn, would date more than one guy at a time because of the excitement of sneaking around and not getting caught.

These guys only brought hurt, low self-esteem and abuse to our relationships. God was showing me that I needed to try a new type of a guy. A one-woman type of guy that was emotionally stable enough to be consistent in the daily monotony of life.

That weekend changed my life forever! Being able to re-visit my past by journaling and evaluating each guy was a painful process but something I had to do. This brought healing, peace, and a release of each soul tie I had with every single guy from my past. A soul-tie is an unhealthy connection to someone that keeps you from loving God and others in a healthy way.

Past wounds are like "owies" you got as a child when you fell down and scraped your knees. When the wound was fresh, it hurts badly. When mom cleaned it up, it stung but she said, "It will get worse if I don't clean it up." So you let her pour on the hydrogen peroxide. OUCH! She usually left the wound open so it would heal faster, although sometimes she put a band-aid over it, so nothing would bother or irritate it. As the wound healed, it turned into a scab. If you picked at the scab, it made it worse. It would start bleeding and sometimes got infected. After it finally healed, you had a cool scar to show off to your friends.

This is the same way with emotional wounds. When you first get hurt or disappointed, it hurts really bad. You might have turned to drugs or alcohol to stop the pain, even if it's for a little while. What you need is to let Jesus help clean it up so the wound can start healing. You need to be open and freely talk about it so the wound will heal even faster. If you let it get bottled up inside, the wound may stay there for a long time.

You cannot keep going back to that wound and dwelling on it because that will be like picking at the scab that prevents it from healing properly. Finally, the emotional scar that is left from the wound will remind you how you once were in bondage, but now you are healed and you

He heals the brokenhearted and binds up their wounds –
Psalms 147:3

can testify of God's love and grace that healed your wounds. You can show your scars to others to let them know of the healing power through Jesus. Sharing your testimony will give hope to others that are going through the same issues that you have overcome.

My God truly healed my bitter and broken heart during that self-retreat with him. Sometimes you just need to get alone with God with no distractions, so you can hear his voice again. It's amazing how you can hear God more when you are still, instead of constantly moving and being distracted by so many things around you. BE STILL!

9

POTENTIAL PROSPECT

"Qualifications"

Now that you have identified relationship patterns from your past, you must determine your qualifications for potential prospects. Write down what qualifications you want in a godly mate. Maybe before you became a Born-Again Virgin, looks were an important quality that you required. You need to ask yourself why looks are so important to you. What will happen if you base your relationship on looks and God forbid, that person gets in a car crash? Will you dump that person because he doesn't have that good looking face anymore? You must think differently than you used to when you were being influenced by the world. Seek God to help you discover what qualities God wants for you, not what you think you want.

Let me share with you of a time that looks was still so important to me. I was very attracted to this guy at church. He was so handsome that I just had to get to know him. We went out a lot as "friends only", but I wanted more because he was so handsome! I thought he was a potential prospect for me. Of course I would pray about it and hoping God would tell me this was my mate for life. But instead God gave me a vision.

I was standing at a crossroad. The path to the left had this handsome guy waiting for me with the 2.5 kids, dog, car and house with a white picket fence. I only had to take a few steps out and I would be there. This would be a dream come true. Something I've always dreamed of as a little girl. But then when I look to the right, that path didn't look so inviting. It was a long narrow dirt road that led out to the horizon. If I squinted, I can see a castle in a far distance. The road look long and I didn't know what to expect once I reached this castle. I could either be one of the servant girls or be the queen of the castle.

As I stood there at the crossroad, I thought I can take the path on the left, have my dream husband, family & life then take the back roads to get to the castle. It may take longer, but at least I would eventually get there. I tried to analyze to manipulate it where I can get both of these dreams. But who was I fooling? I knew this guy was no good for me because it was just a physical attraction.

I knew which road God wanted me to take and I was just being stubborn because I wanted it my way. I did make the decision to take the long narrow road. After I made this decision, I told this handsome guy that God wanted me to take a break from dating and hanging out so much with guys. Do you know that it wasn't even two weeks later, he started dating someone else? That was heartbreaking. But I know I made the right decision.

Ladies, look at the examples in the Bible of godly men and not-so godly men. First let's check out Samson. What woman wouldn't want someone as good looking and strong as Samson? He sounds like every woman's dream. But look at his character (Judges 16). From the beginning he chased after women that did not love God.

His parents even tried to stop him but he wanted Philistine women. I am not saying that it's bad to like good-looking guys. I am saying that first and foremost, you must not be with someone who is not a believer (2 Corinthians 6:14).

Think about it. If you are with a guy that is not a believer, you most likely will go to church alone and not be able to have conversations about God. Sooner or later, it will bring a big wedge into the relationship.

I knew a lady that was married to an unbeliever. She could talk to him about anything but God. She was not allowed to listen to Christian music when he was at home or in the car with her. She couldn't study her Bible or read Christian books when he was around. She was a prisoner in her own home. It was a very sad situation.

> *Do not be yoked together with unbelievers. For what do righteousness and wickedness have in common? Or what fellowship can light have with darkness?*
> *2 Corinthians 6:14.*

So now let's turn to a godly man in the Bible. Let's look at Joseph. He was well-built and handsome like Samson but look what he did in the situation with his Master's wife in **Genesis 39:7, 8** – *his master's wife took notice of Joseph and said, "Come to bed with me!"* But he refused. Not only because she was his master's wife but because he states in verse 9, *"How then could I do such a wicked thing and sin against God?"* He did not want to sin against God, even when she continued to try to get him to sleep with her day in and day out. Joseph did the opposite of Samson. Which one would you choose as a godly man?

Now, what about the women in the bible? Let's check out Delilah. Sure, she may have had the looks and the charm to persuade Samson, but look where that got him. The challenge may have been exciting at first but the thrill led to his death. Are you being deceptive by flirting with men and leading them down the path of destruction? Ungodly women will use their looks or body to get something in return from a guy.

The supermodel of the bible is Esther! Can you tell by now that I love the story of Esther? Once again, she is the example of a godly woman. Esther didn't go flirting or sneaking around with other guys. She stayed focus on preparing herself for her king. She loved God and she wasn't going to settle for less. She wanted God's best in her life.

"For my thoughts are not your thoughts, neither are your ways my ways", declares the Lord. "As the heavens are higher than the earth, so are My ways higher than your ways and My thoughts than your thoughts". Isaiah 55:8,9

So who are you? A Delilah or an Esther? Review the type of men that you are attracting. Are they like flies that you keep having to swat away? If so, then make a simple change so you can attract exceptional prospects. The secret is to be ultimately preparing yourself for Jesus. You don't have to try to find your mate or think every guy that comes along is a prospect. Stay focus on Jesus and watch the elite be attracted to you. This will not be based on your outward beauty, but the inward beauty that Jesus will bring forth out of you.

Be aware of guys that are looking for that trophy wife only. Okay, so what happens when you have children and gravity takes hold of your body? You bore the pain of having his children and then he is ready to trade you in for a new trophy wife. No one can ever be that perfect trophy wife. So, stop trying so hard! Don't put that much pressure on yourself.

Ladies, I have great news for you! It goes beyond appearance. You need to look deep into the heart of potential prospects. Things to look for are godly traits like integrity, generosity, and gentleness. In addition, you must give a reason why you want a certain quality in your future mate. Never base it on looks alone.

Pick out three top qualities, which you feel are the most important. Once you have your top qualities, pray to see which qualities God would choose for you. Compare your choices with God's. Do they match? If not, I suggest you choose God's ways over your own because he will make better choices for you than you will make for yourself.

Time-Out #11

A. List top qualities you look for in a mate and explain why:

1. _____

    Why: _____

2. _____

    Why: _____

3. _____

    Why: _____

4. _____

    Why: _____

5. _____

    Why: _____

6. _____

    Why: _____

7. _____

    Why: _____

8. _____

    Why: _____

9. _____

    Why: _____

B.   List *your* top 3 important qualities from the above list:

1. _____
2. _____
3. _____

C.   List the top 3 qualities from the above list that you think *God would choose (should NOT be the same as your top 3)*:

1. _____
2. _____
3. _____

Now, turn the table around. What qualities do you have to offer to someone? Pick the top three positive qualities you feel you have to offer. What qualities do you think God would say are your strengths? Remember that the best way to attract someone is to be attractive yourself. Work on being the kind of person God wants you to be and you will be the kind of person others want to be around.

Time-Out #12

A. List top qualities you feel that YOU HAVE to offer someone:

1. _____

    Why: _____

2. _____

    Why: _____

3. _____

    Why: _____

4. _____

    Why: _____

5. _____

    Why: _____

6. _____

    Why: _____

7. _____

    Why: _____

8. _____

    Why: _____

9. _____

    Why: _____

A. List *your* top 3 qualities you feel you have to offer from the above list:

    1) _____

    2) _____

    3) _____

B. List the top 3 qualities from the above list that you think *God would choose (should NOT be your top 3)*:

    1) _____

    2) _____

    3) _____

C. Compare what you have to offer with the qualities that you want in someone:

Similarities

    ➢ _____

    ➢ _____

    ➢ _____

Differences

    ➢ _____

    ➢ _____

    ➢ _____

Considering what type of godly mate you want to be with will prevent you from getting caught up with the first person that shows an interest in you. Check to see how that person lines up with the qualities you and God have chosen. Don't settle for less. I love a quote I once heard from a preacher, "Good is the enemy of Best." You can settle for Good but it may not necessarily be the Best. You decide!

10

UNDER GOD'S CONSTRUCTION

"Re-building From A Sure Foundation"

Remember the nursery story of the three little pigs? The first two pigs got their house blown down by the big bad wolf. But the third little pig built his house on a firm foundation so it didn't get blown down. You can save yourself a lot of headaches and disappointments if you just learn from others, instead of always doing it your own way.

It may have taken the third pig a little longer to build his house but he did it the right way and it paid off in the end. So what can you learn when your life is a wreck like the two pigs? You must learn to re-build on a solid foundation like the third pig. Your sure foundation is Jesus. He is the solid rock you can build your life on.

You need to stand firm in Jesus as it states in **1 Peter 5:10 – "And the God of all grace, who called you to his eternal glory in Christ, after you have suffered a little while, will himself restore you and make you strong, firm and steadfast."** Maybe you've made mistakes. And the enemy is telling you how you have blown it too much for God to help. That is so far from the truth! What the enemy meant for evil, God wants to turn around for good, but you have to be willing to let him re-structure your life.

Let's take a look at another nursery rhyme, Humpty Dumpty. Did you ever wonder what Humpty Dumpty was doing up on that wall anyway? Humpty Dumpty was an egg. Eggs are fragile. They should be kept in safe places like egg cartons, not sitting up on high walls. Apparently Humpty Dumpty forgot about his limitations, ignored the dangers around him, and put himself into a risky situation. Humpty Dumpy was an

Pride goes before destruction and a haughty spirit before a fall.
Proverbs 16:18

accident just waiting to happen. Imagine with me for a moment an arrogant Humpty Dumpty dancing and showing off until he ended up having a "great fall." SPLAT!

Let's discover how his life relates to yours. Have you ever felt like you were at the peak of your success, and just as you were showing off and getting conceited, something causes you to fall just like Humpty Dumpty? Let's get a little bit more personal. Maybe you were living your happily-ever-after-Cinderella marriage. Then one day, your spouse left you for someone else and your *DREAM* was shattered into pieces. Maybe you had a good childhood until one day that uncle or stepfather molested you and your *SOUL* was shattered into pieces. Maybe you had a great family life until one day, your parent became very ill and died and your *FAMILY* came tumbling down into pieces. Have you found yourselves in a thousand pieces at one time or another? Maybe you are there now. No one is exempt from having their lives shatter into pieces.

When an egg is cracked open, who can put it back together again? Just like Humpty Dumpty, all the king's horses and all the king's men couldn't put him back together again. No one on this earth can put your shattered pieces back together. The only answer is a miracle from God. Only Jesus can pick up the pieces and rebuild from the inside out. He makes you whole again by restructuring your life.

What is broken in your life? Maybe it's a broken spirit, broken family, broken relationship, broken home, or broken friendship. The Bible says in *Psalm 5:17, "...a broken and contrite heart, O God, you will not despise."* This means that God will not turn you away. He can mend a broken heart. That may not necessarily mean you will get back together with your ex-spouse or ex-boyfriend. It means God will restructure YOU.

I remember a time when my heart was shattered into pieces. I got married at 19 years old and divorced a few years later. I got saved shortly after that. As I studied the Bible, I realized that God hates divorce. I kept hearing sermons and people talking about God bringing reconciliation in marriages, even after divorce.

My ex-husband and I were still friends. I thought God wanted us back together. I prayed and told God that I was open to getting back together with my ex-husband. Not even two weeks after that prayer, I got a couple of collect calls from my ex-husband. It was strange because he kept hanging up after I accepted his collect calls. Shortly after that, I was at his cousin's baby shower and noticed a wedding ring on his finger. My heart sank and I was crushed! That was God's way of closing the door that I thought I was supposed to go through again. At that time, I was hurt and I couldn't understand why God did that since the Bible says God hates divorce.

At first you may think that your prayers are not answered because you don't get what you want. But in time, you will begin to understand why God answers prayers the way he does. It is always for your best interest even though you may not see it that way. It took me over fifteen years to rebuild my life and redefine who I was as a child of God before God brought my mate for life.

During that time, I was under God's construction. He showed me things about myself that I never realized before such as being too afraid to go anywhere alone, particularly where there were other couples around. But God showed me that I wasn't alone. He was right there with me. So whenever I went places, I would talk to God just like talking to a friend. I even got to the point, where I was able to go to a restaurant by myself to eat. I didn't necessarily carry a conversation with myself out loud, as I didn't want people to think I was really crazy. But within my heart, I would talk to God and sitting alone at a restaurant didn't bother me anymore.

Let him show you how awesome it is to be wined and dined by the Lover of your soul! No other person on earth will treat you as well as God can. When you understand that he is your everything, you will not need anything or anyone else. Did you hear that? I said need, not want. You might want this or that, but he knows what you need. Plus, he owns everything on earth and desires to share it all with you! Be open to him and he will sweep you off your feet like no one in this world can!

For example, I realized I was jealous when other females received roses from guys, so I planted a bunch of roses in my yard and thanked God for them whenever they blossomed. After all, he is the Creator of everything and he made them blossom just for me! God gave me more roses than any one guy could afford! When people saw the flowers on my tabletop, they would ask who gave them to me. My response would be, "My lover, Jesus, the lover of my soul." It's all about perspective.

The next time you feel lonely, try letting Jesus romance you like no one else can. Instead of focusing on what you are missing, let him open your eyes to what you already have. Open your heart to Jesus and he will show you that you don't have to wait until you get to your destination to enjoy life. If you stop and smell the roses along the way, you will enjoy the journey, too!

Consider yourself at this time under construction. Let God remodel your ideas about singleness and he will blow your socks off with blessings! Let him rebuild your life on the foundation of his promises.

> *Humble yourselves, therefore, under God's mighty hand, that He may lift you up in due time.*
> *1 Peter 5:6*

You might be afraid to wait for God to fulfill his promises because so many others have broken their promises to you. That's understandable, but don't let fear keep you from enjoying the benefits of God's perfect love and timing. Think about it. Maybe God is waiting to bring your mate because that person isn't ready yet. Maybe there are issues that you need to work on before you're ready for a committed relationship.

> *For this reason a man will leave his father and mother and be united to his wife and they will become one flesh. The man and his wife were both naked, and they felt no shame.*
> *Genesis 2:24-25*

One of the issues I had to work on was shame. In Genesis 2:24-

25, it says Adam and Eve felt no shame in being naked. When you come together in a marriage covenant as husband and wife, there is no shame in being naked with each other. I have to say I have truly experienced this with my husband now, although it hasn't always been like this. In the past, I was so ashamed of my body. I used to only have sex in the dark and didn't like being naked other than in the shower.

When Mike and I first got married, I was very shy when it came to being naked around him. He was confident about himself and didn't have a problem being naked. As we became one flesh and I came to know who I was in Christ and as a Christian wife, I overcame the feeling of shame whenever I was naked. This is even after gaining 30 pounds! Now that is a victory to shout about. HALLELUJAH!

God saw all that He had made, and it was very good.

Genesis 1:31

Remember that you are made in God's image and when you don't like yourself, particularly your body; you are putting down what God created. You may see flaws in your own body, but in God's eyes you are perfect. Embrace the fact that God loves you just the way you are. Ask Him to show you how he sees your body as beautiful. You are uniquely made by him and he made everything good.

I can honestly say that even though I have been with a lot of men in my life. By far, my husband is the best sexual relationship I've ever experienced. It is beyond my wildest imagination that sex can be this great. When you make Christ the center of your marriage, it will be the best ever!

Because of bad experiences with sexual relationships in my past, I viewed sex as bad and dirty. Do you perceive sex as being bad and only done in the dark and in secret? I used to think that God would never approve of sex. I finally realized that doesn't make sense because it is God who created sex in the first place. Unfortunately, many of us have experienced sex in ways God never intended. God's perfect plan is for one man and one woman to commit to each other for life in a marriage relationship. Did you hear that? Sex is not bad if it's in a marriage relationship between a male and a female.

Instead of praying for God to take away your sexual desires, pray for insight, courage and wisdom in restraining those desires during this season of singleness. Believe me, once you are married, you will want those sexual desires. It will be a blessing to your mate. But right now, you will need to exercise self-control and discipline especially in your mind. If you can get your mind under control, your body will follow suit.

I have mentioned several fears I had to face in order to be content as a Christian single adult and to prepare myself for my mate. I had to deal with the fear of rejection, the fear of being alone, and the fear of being naked. What are some of your fears?

Time-Out #13

Some Fears I have about being single:

➢ _____

_____

➢ _____

_____

➢ _____

_____

➢ _____

_____

➢ _____

_____

➢ _____

_____

One way to overcome fear is to fight it with Bible verses. For instance, if you are afraid of being alone you could memorize Hebrews 13:5 - *"Never will I leave you; never will I forsake you."* Now apply this to yourself and quote back, "God will never leave me or forsake me, therefore, I am never alone. He is always with me." Each time you find a way to overcome your fear, you are on your way to victory!

PRAYER

Dear Heavenly Father,

I come humbly before you with the fears I have about being single (say out loud the fears you wrote). I ask that you help me overcome these fears, for the bible says that You did not give us a spirit of fear, but of love, power and a sound mind. Holy Spirit, show me things about myself that I need to work on during this time of being under your construction. Most of all, teach me how to enjoy being single during this season of my life.

In Jesus Name,

Amen.

Vilma Conner

11

BEAUTY FOR ASHES

"Spiritual Make-Over"

> (v1) The Spirit of the Sovereign Lord is on me, because the Lord has anointed me to preach good news to the poor. He has sent me to bind up the brokenhearted, to proclaim freedom for the captives and release from darkness for the prisoners. (v2) To proclaim the year of the Lord's favor and the day of vengeance of our God, to comfort all who mourn, and provide those who grieve in Zion – (v3) To bestow on them a crown of beauty instead of ashes, the oil of gladness instead of mourning, and a garment of praise instead of a spirit of despair. They will be called oaks of righteousness, a planting of the LORD for the display of His splendor.
>
> Isaiah 61:1-3

As a Born-Again Virgin, you have access to God's spiritual makeover described in Isaiah 61. It's like having a free pass to the best spa ever. The first thing you need in your spiritual make-over is *favor* (verse 2).

Let's look at the story of Mary, the mother of Jesus, in Luke 1:28-38. An angel came to her and told her she was "highly favored" by God and then told her that God was going to replace her ordinary dreams with extraordinary blessings! I'm sure before the angel came to her, Mary had the typical Cinderella fairy tale dream of getting married, having children and living happily ever after. This is an *"Ordinary Dream"* that girls have. But when the angel came to her, it was a *"Defining Moment"* in Mary's life where she had to make a decision. Did she want to accept the extraordinary blessing that God had planned for her or did she want to stay with the ordinary dream that every girl her age dreamed?

Look at verse 34 where she asked, "How will this be since I am a virgin?" In her mind, it did not add up. Two plus two did not equal seven. In verse 37, the angel said, "FOR NOTHING IS IMPOSSIBLE WITH GOD!" I love Mary's faith because her response in verse 38 was, "May it be to me as you have said." Because she accepted what God chose for her life, even though it made no sense in her logical mind, she enjoyed the extraordinary blessings of having a special bond with Jesus.

God will not force you to do something you don't want to do. You need to respond the same way Mary did. If God has something extraordinary for you to do in life, your response should be, **"BRING IT ON, GOD."** What if God is calling you to be the next preacher like Joyce Meyer or TD Jakes? You may be thinking, no way, I don't know how to preach or know enough about the Bible. That's okay. All you have to do is be willing and say, "I don't know how this is going to take place Lord, but here I am, willing and available for whatever you have for me."

Back in 1994 when I became a Christian I never dreamed that I would be on stage speaking to crowds as I do today. I knew my calling and purpose in life was to help young and hurting women. I even had a vision that I would be speaking to hundreds and thousands of young people. I never thought I could do it because I always had a fear about speaking in public. Plus I never thought I was dynamic or interesting enough. In my mind, I thought I would help people on a one-on-one basis, which in turn would add up to hundreds and thousands of people over time. When I surrendered my ordinary life and chose to be "highly favored" with God's extraordinary blessing, he gave me the courage and the opportunities to speak in front of people.

When God gives you a vision, don't sell yourself short saying that it can never happen. The scripture says, *"For nothing is impossible with God."* As Born-Again Virgins, we are bold, we are blessed and we are highly favored by the most high God. We just have to receive and accept it. AMEN!

Let's continue your spiritual makeover by putting on a crown of beauty instead of ashes (Isaiah 61:3). In Bible times, it was a custom for people to put ashes on their heads as a sign of mourning. It was also common to sit in a pile of ashes. Job was known for sitting in a pile of ashes when he was going through his hardship of losing everything and everyone in his life.

When something is burned, ashes come from it, which is nothing more than the remains of something that once was. It reminds you of what was there. For example if a house burns down, there are ashes from the fire that remain until it is cleaned up.

Are you still lying in the pile of ashes from the past? Have you been burnt by betrayal, abandonment, verbal or physical abuse, or divorce? Are you mourning your loss of innocence because of molestation, incest or rape? Isaiah 61:2 says Jesus came to comfort all who mourn and give you beauty for those ashes.

The Hebrew word for beauty could be translated as "Embellishment.' God wants to pick you up out of the ashes and make something beautiful of your life embellishing it with his favor and blessing. God still sees you as beautiful because he is looking at your heart. Think of how profound this is. With God, you don't have to hide your blemishes under heavy make-up afraid that he will reject you if you're not pretty enough. He sees the true beauty that comes from within.

Let's continue with the spiritual make-over and apply the oil of gladness instead of mourning. There were different types of oil in the Bible such as anointing oil, oil for medical purposes, and oils used for beauty treatment (as in Esther). Oil was even applied to the face to make the face shine (maybe like makeup today). When people where in mourning, no oil would be applied to the face so that people would know when someone was in mourning.

Mourning deals with grief, sorrow, sadness, hurt, or pain from the past. This has to do mostly with your emotions. Are you are grieving about something that has happened to you? Maybe you're grieving a past relationship that has failed or past memories of losing a loved one through death, rejection, abandonment, or abortion.

When I first committed my life to God, I was on a spiritual high and life was good. But then as I matured in my relationship with God, hurts started to surface from my past. As I mentioned earlier, issues came up with my biological father. Even though I never knew him, the issues of rejection and abandonment surfaced.

I used to ask myself why a father would leave a child that was sick and could have died. At two years old, I caught Polio in the Philippines and was very sick.

My biological father was never there for me. He didn't even help my mom financially.

Although this happened to me as a toddler, it carried over into my adult life when it came to relationships with men. Subconsciously, I had a fear of rejection. God showed me that even though my biological father was never a father to me I do have a Heavenly Father and he will never reject or abandon me. He loves me and meets all my needs.

"I will never leave you nor forsake you."

Joshua 1:6
and
Hebrews 13:5

God wants to give you gladness for your past sorrows. Happiness is determined by the circumstances around you. It is external. Joy comes from the Lord and is internal. You can have the joy of the Lord even when the circumstances around you are bad.

The garment of praise instead of a spirit of despair is your next item for a spiritual make-over. Let's first look at the spirit of despair. Despair means to lose all hope or confidence. It includes heaviness, depression, hopelessness, suicidal tendencies, and self-pity. The root of this spirit of heaviness can come from bitterness, unforgiveness or even ingratitude.

King Saul was affected by depression. He called for David to play and sing the anointed Psalms. God's word and music calmed King Saul's spirit. There is something about the presence of God that calms the spirit. He will give you peace and joy when you choose to praise him. In Hebrew the word **"Tehillah"** means to sing praise. Note that it is not tequila, but tehillah. Maybe in your past you did a lot of tequila, but now you need to switch over to a lot of tehillah!

Every morning you decide what to wear. In the same way you must decide to put on the garment of praise and not the spirit of despair. What you wear often tells about your mood. When you go to a funeral, you wear black. Typically black is a color of clothing that is serious and somber. You don't see many people wearing Hawaiian shirts to funerals. When you think of a Hawaiian shirt, you think of something very fun, colorful and uplifting.

What Jesus does is take our black clothes of despair and give us clothes of praise. Praise prepares us for miracles and blessings in our lives. Psalm 22:3 says God inhabits the praises of his people. Not only does God love it when we praise him, but it uplifts our spirit. This makes us feel good from the inside out. God wants to replace our miseries with praise.

Now that you've had your spiritual makeover, imagine yourself wearing a beautiful gold crown instead of ashes and a royal robe of praise rather than the rags of despair. See yourself shining with gladness. Can you see yourself this way? You have to visualize yourself as a princess. Once you do, then you can start acting like one! The last part of Isaiah 61:3 describes God's followers as "Oaks of righteousness." As a Born-Again Virgin, your life should reflect God's goodness and be a "Display of his splendor."

You may feel like your life is ugly and insignificant. Remember the story of the ugly duckling. It felt that it didn't fit in with the other ducks. But what happened as it matured? It became a beautiful swan – more beautiful than the ducks it used to hang out with. Now that you are a Born-Again Virgin, you are a beautiful swan. Don't be surprised when you no longer fit in with the ducks you used to hang out with. God is making you different from the inside out. Others will notice it and will start responding differently to you. Resist the urge to go back to your old ways of flirting or trading sex for affection. Stand strong in your spiritual makeover and be an oak of righteousness. In time, you and those around you will get used to the dignity and respect you deserve as a beautiful swan.

Let's take some time out to study the oak tree. The oak tree starts as a seed called an acorn. The chances of one acorn making it to become an oak tree is very slim. It is 1 in 10,000 acorns. That means that for every 10,000 acorns, only one will become a tree!

There are a lot of reasons why acorns do not make it. Little insects called weevils bore into acorns to deposit their eggs, which mature in spring. Up to 90% of the acorns in a region can be destroyed by the larvae of the weevils. Squirrels, blue jays, woodpeckers, deers and wild turkeys eat acorns. Another enemy is mold. When oak trees shed their leaves during the autumn, they end up covering the acorns. The thick, moist blanket of leaves is a breeding ground for mold.

As you can see, acorns are vulnerable. Let's look at how this relates to your spiritual makeover. First, getting involved with a good Bible-based church will protect you from the spiritual weevil of selfishness. Being plugged into a group will teach you Christian principles like love, forgiveness, and gratitude. This is a process that takes time. You cannot rush it.

Staying in a church will also teach you to guard yourself against things that will eat you alive as a Born-Again Virgin. Lying, cheating, and gossiping are like those squirrels that eat acorns for breakfast. Solid Christian friendships will also act like leave blowers. To keep yourself from getting covered up in your old ways and developing "mold" that can destroy new growth, you'll have to maintain open, honest relationships with other Born-Again Virgins who are committed to living for God.

These are things you need to be careful of if you want to become that mature oak of righteousness that God is talking about in Isaiah 61:3. He wants to display you as his splendor. In other words, he wants to show you off so you can make a difference in other people's lives with your testimony and the changed life that you have in Christ.

Do you really want to be that strong oak for God? If you do, here are some simple steps to follow:

1. It starts with your PAST. Surrender your past and your old ways to God.

2. In your PRESENT, let him fill you with Beauty, Gladness and Praise right now where you are at.

3. Be like that acorn and plant yourself in a Bible-based Church, to that you will grow into a mature, solid "Oak of righteousness".

4. Enjoy your new makeover! God has made you a "Display of His splendor".

PART III

Ready, Set, GO!

12

DON'T WORRY
BE HAPPY

"Being Content"

Contentment is another C-word that singles have a hard time with. I know I did. I didn't really know what it meant to be content for most of my single life. I thought I was content and even told people that I was content. I kept speaking it out trying to convince myself that I was. Yet, inside I knew I was unhappy because I was not married yet. This mind-set led me into thoughts of self-pity, anger and frustration.

The hardest time of the year for me started with the Thanksgiving Holiday, carried through to Christmas, onto New Years, through my birthday in January and then Valentine's Day in February. These four months were the toughest for me as a single adult.

During the holidays, I had family members always asking me why I was not married yet? All my brothers were married with children. The number of nieces and nephews kept growing every year. I was the oldest and I was afraid I was going to be the aunt that takes in all the stray cats from the neighborhood, the old maid that has to keep animals around to keep her company. Because of this, I never liked cats!

I hated the feeling of not having that special someone to spoil me for my birthday, or even worse, no one to share a romantic Valentine's Day with. It took me years to realize that these four months were constantly miserable for me. Finally, I made up my mind (with God's help of course) that I wasn't going to be down and depressed during these months anymore. It was a choice I had to make because I wanted to get out of the rut I stayed in. I was tired of being unhappy four months out of every year.

Because I changed my mind-set, my answer became different when family members asked why I wasn't married yet. I told them I was waiting for God to bring that special someone and I was willing to wait until he thought I was ready. I told them to take it up with God if they thought He was moving too slow. It shut them up pretty quick. I even started enjoying my visits with my nieces and nephews instead of wishing I had kids of my own. Getting through the holidays with this type of attitude gave me confidence that I didn't know I had.

I thought my birthday would be the toughest day for God to redeem. But after spending time in prayer and keeping this new mind-set, it wasn't so bad. I cooked a nice dinner for myself and I had a lovely time at home with God. I had such a peace in my heart that I actually enjoyed a night at home. In the past, I would have called a friend to take me out for my birthday.

Then Valentine's Day came - the most dreaded day of all! This was the toughest, but I knew I had to change my attitude. This day represents affection and love towards someone. What better way than to express my affection and love to my one and only-JESUS!

I even had the courage to go out with another couple as a third wheel on Valentine's Day. Before, I wouldn't even go near a restaurant on that day because so many lovebirds were out celebrating, but the confidence God gave me brought me peace and I was truly okay with this day.

I came to the realization that if I was to remain single for the rest of my life, so be it. I was truly okay with it in my heart. It wasn't just talk anymore. I was enjoying life with my God and I was content with that. Do you know that a few months later, God brought my mate for life? I really believe it was because I was truly content in my heart and God knew that. It was as though I could hear him say, "Aahh, you finally got it! Okay, now you are ready," and SHAZAM! Out of nowhere, God brings me my mate.

> *I am not saying this because I am in need, for I have learned to be content whatever the circumstances. I know what it is to be in need, and I know what it is to have plenty. I have learned the secret of being content in any and every situation, whether well fed or hungry, whether living in plenty or in want. I can do everything through him who gives me strength.*
> *Philippians 4:11-13*

I truly learned to be content in my heart. The key here is "learned". It's not a natural thing. I had to learn it from the Holy Spirit. I have to say, when I was finally content with being single, God threw a curve ball at me. I didn't see it coming.

Mike and I had been working together for a year. I saw his heart and passion for ministry and people. However, I never entertained the thought of a relationship with him. When I heard he was interested in me, I even tried to set him up with a friend of mine. I thought they had more in common with each other. I wanted them to be happy. At this point in my life, I was enjoying my singleness so much that I didn't want to waste my time with a relationship.

I remember I was sick for about a week and a friend told me I was probably making myself sick being in denial over Mike. Everyone around me knew we were made for each other. My friend asked me if I had prayed about it. I told my friend I didn't have to, I knew Mike wasn't the one for me. But, my friend challenged me to open myself up to the possibility that this was God's will.

So I prayed and do you know how God responded? Remember my prayer earlier in Chapter 2 of this book. It was time for God to answer this prayer.

GOD, PLEASE...

1. Guard my heart
2. Not my will, but Yours be done
3. Give my heart to my mate because I always give my heart out to the wrong guys. *(The choices I made usually ended up hurting me)*

God brought this prayer back to my remembrance. He responded this way:

> *God said, "Didn't you say to guard your heart"*
>
> My response, "Yes."
>
> *God said, "Didn't you say not your will, but Mine be done"*
>
> My response, "Yes."
>
> *God said, "Didn't you say that you wanted Me to choose the guy who is safe to give your heart to?"*
>
> My response, "Yes."
>
> *God said, "So what's the PROBLEM?"*

Wow, it was like a brick hit me upside the head. And the rest is history! So be careful what you pray for. God will give it to you, in his time, of course, even when his timing seems longer than ours. God is in no hurry. He takes his time to make sure everything is made beautiful.

He has made everything beautiful in His time.
Ecclesiastes 3:11

Being single can bring contentment if you let it. If you keep desiring to be married, you will miss out on your life right now. The bottom line is that on your worst day being single, you have God and you are still going to heaven. Can you imagine if you didn't have God in your life or the promise of eternity with him? Many singles in this world don't have what you have! They don't have hope or any promises for the rest of their lives. It could be a lot worse out there. Stop feeling sorry for yourself and start living life to the fullest! You can do it only with God. Relax and enjoy this journey of singleness.

A misunderstood C-word is celebration. It's hard to be happy for someone else that finds their soul mate when you have been waiting for 10, 15 or maybe even 20 years. It's not fair, you say? You are right. It's not. But hey, that is part of life. Get over it or you will be miserable. What's worse is you will start affecting others around you and make them miserable, too. No one will want to be around you and then you will be lonely and single for even longer.

You cannot control circumstances around you; however, you can control how you respond. When your friend, or better yet, your enemy gets engaged, are you happy for them or do you complain? Why is it always someone else? That should have been me. When is it going to be *MY* turn? Believe me; this attitude is not pleasing to God. No wonder he hasn't brought anyone your way.

I was in the same boat with my complaining, sourpuss friends, quoting that famous saying "Always the bridesmaid, never the bride." ***"DO NOT COVET",*** is one of the Ten Commandments. In Romans 13:9 it says to "Love your neighbor, as yourself." You need to learn to love others and not covet what they have. Coveting will only lead to bitterness and resentment in your heart. Love will bring peace and joy in your heart. The choice is yours. Let me ask you this, when God makes that wedding day happen for you, don't you want everyone celebrating with you? Or would you rather have a bunch of your single friends complaining?

If you want people to rejoice and celebrate at your wedding, well guess what? YOU must rejoice and celebrate at theirs. Put your selfishness aside and be the biggest supporter of the person getting married.

> *Whoever sows sparingly will also reap sparingly and whoever sows generously will also reap generously.*
>
> *2 Corinthians 9:6*

Look at the story of the prodigal son in Luke 15:11-32. Read the passage if you are not familiar with it. When the prodigal son came back home, his father had a big celebration for him. What does his brother do when he comes home from a hard day at work? He is angry and complains how he had been faithful in working hard for his father and his father has never thrown him a big party. If anyone deserves a party, it should have been the brother that has been faithful. In verse 32, the father said, "But we had to celebrate and be glad." This is what your heavenly Father wants you to do when others are blessed, even if you think they do not deserve it. It is right that you rejoice and celebrate with your friends and enemies when it's their time to get married! If you do this for others, it will be done for you when it is your turn.

 ### _Time-Out #14_

Here are some ways to celebrate with others:

- ➢ Send a card or e-card congratulating them on their engagement/wedding.
- ➢ Be happy and encourage them in words/scriptures each time you see them in person.
- ➢ Pray for them as individuals, their marriage and future together.

- ➢ Keep the focus on them. Don't make them feel sorry for you for not having someone.
- ➢ Other: _____
  _____
- ➢ Other: _____
  _____
- ➢ Other: _____
  _____

Celebrate good times, come on! Celebration can go hand-in-hand with contentment. You will notice that the more you celebrate with others, the more you will have those mountain-top experiences of contentment.

Stop and review all the times you could have had a good time but chose to complain instead. Celebrate with others every chance you get. It will not only bless them, but you will be blessed as well! What are you waiting on? Get out there and celebrate!

Vilma Conner

13

REPORT CARD

"Measuring Your Progress"

It's time to measure your progress. In school, you are graded on how well you are learning various subjects. You usually receive a report card every quarter. As a Born-Again Virgin, you need to do the same. Every few months, you need to grade yourself on your progress with accountability partners, your thought life, boundaries, commitments, your sabbatical year, your fears, your level of contentment, and your ability to celebrate.

When it comes to measuring your progress with your accountability partners, you need to look at how often you keep in contact with them. Are you discussing issues with your accountability partners or just keeping to small talk? You need to evaluate with your accountability partner where you are at with the things you listed in your accountability partnership agreement. If you are not keeping your accountability partner informed on a regular basis, chances are you aren't progressing in the area of accountability.

Measuring boundaries is a vital to survive on this journey! If you compromise in this area, you could fall hard! Boundaries are set to keep you safe. Keep in mind the boundaries you set for yourself with your time, emotions, and in physical areas. Little compromises can get you into big trouble. Keeping boundaries intact will help prevent those little compromises that turn into big problems for Born-Again Virgins.

If you are serious about your commitments to God, you will keep your word not only to him, but to others. Check yourself to see if you are following through with your commitments to God, to your family and even to yourself. Be a person of your word.

Your thought life is the next thing to measure. Remember the Time-Out exercise in Chapter 5, the "Whatever things." The first thing on this list is "true" things. Are you thinking about the true things of God or are you thinking the about false things of the world? Be honest with yourself and with God. Get your thought life under control.

Are you on a roller-coaster ride with contentment? Do you have the mountain-top experience with contentment than within minutes, come crashing down? When you find yourself on this roller-coaster ride, hang on and press through. It says in Job 36:11 that if you obey and serve God, you will spend the rest of your days in prosperity and your years in contentment.

You have to do your part in obeying and serving, and then God's promise to you will be fulfilled. Remember that you have just started this Born-Again Virgin journey and it takes time to learn to be content. You will get there. Don't give up in this area! Keep pressing through.

Sometimes, you won't do so well on your Born-Again Virgin report card. If you are failing in a certain area, don't get discouraged. It's better to be honest about it so you can correct yourself by getting back to the basics. Reread the chapters that pertain to your struggle. Don't be afraid to start over. God is a God of second, third, fourth, fifth chances.

To keep track of your grades throughout your journey, check out the following website:

Internet Interactive Website: **www.bavirgin.com**
Book Entry Keyword: **REPORT CARD**

Let me give you a big tip to help you get better grades on your report card. Create a blessing box. You ask, what is a blessing box? First, let's look at the story of the Israelites in Exodus 12:31-32. Pharaoh tells Moses to take the Israelites, along with their flocks and herds, out of Egypt. Even though they were slaves, Pharaoh agreed to give them their freedom and their possessions. That is like being fired from a job but still receiving all the benefits like medical insurance, vacation pay, etc. The Israelites were also blessed when the Lord gave them favor in the sight of their enemies. In verse 35, the Egyptians showered the Israelites with gifts of gold, silver and clothing.

God warned the Israelites to REMEMBER this day. Whenever God blesses you, you need to remember it. If you are like me, you can't even remember what you ate yesterday, let alone last week. I need to write things down to help me remember.

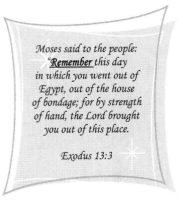

Moses said to the people: "*Remember* this day in which you went out of Egypt, out of the house of bondage; for by strength of hand, the Lord brought you out of this place.

Exodus 13:3

When you receive a blessing from God, write it down and place it in your blessing box. It doesn't have to be in detail. Just write the date with a sentence or two about the blessing. You can make your blessing box out of an old shoe box. You can cover it with nice gift wrapping paper or if you are artistic, you can decorate it as you like. Each time God blesses you, write it down and put it in your blessing box.

If we continue to look at the Israelites on their journey, there were continuous blessings:

➤ God took them on a detour to protect them from their enemies (Exodus 13:17-18).

➢ God led them by giving shade through a cloud during the day and a fire to give them light at night (Exodus 13:21).

➢ God gave them victory over their enemies (Exodus 13:21-31).

➢ God provided food and water (Exodus 15 and 16).

Even with all the blessings God gave, the Israelites continued to complain. Can you relate? When God blesses you, are you all happy? Then when you have a problem, you forget about the blessing that just happened and start complaining. When you are going through a hard time on your journey that is the time when you need to open up your blessing box.

REMEMBER all the blessings that God has given you. You also need to remember that he is not done blessing you yet. Focus on the good things God has done for you knowing that more good things are coming in your future.

Each quarter that you evaluate your progress and grade yourself, get out your blessing box. Each blessing will remind you of God's goodness and love.

This will keep you motivated to move forward on your journey.

14

THE POINT OF "KNOW" RETURN

"Getting Back On Track"

Everyone makes mistakes! It doesn't matter how good you are or how much knowledge you think you have. You will still make mistakes. Sometimes it's what you do after the mistake that makes a difference.

When you are sick, you go to the doctor. When you have legal issues, you go to a lawyer. When you sin, you go straight to God. Don't let the guilt and shame of messing up keep you from God and even stop you from going to church. God already

> *If we confess our sins, he is faithful and just and will forgive us our sins and purify us from all unrighteousness.*
> *1 John 1:9*

knows when you sin. He does not condemn you. He is a loving and merciful God. He is the one that forgives sins. Only with his help can you get back on the right track. When you sin, don't run away from God. Run to him, so that he can help you get back on track.

When you know you are starting to get interested in someone, stop and pray. Evaluate your thoughts, feelings and actions towards this person. Ask for God's help.

PRAYER: **"God, please bring to my mind anything and everything that I have done knowingly or unknowingly that involves _____ (person's name)".** Then ask yourself the following questions:

 Time-Out #15

1. How often do I think of _____ in one day?

   ➤ **Answer:** _____

   _____

   _____

2. When I think of _____, what comes to mind?

   ➤ **Answer:** _____
   _____
   _____

3. How long do I dwell on this?

   ➤ **Answer:** _____
   _____
   _____

4. When I see _____, I feel _____
   _____
   _____

5. The emotions I start feeling are:

   ➤ _____
   _____
   _____
   _____
   _____

When you realize that you think about this person everyday and have feelings towards this person, then you are at the point of "Know" return. Notice it is "Know" and not "No". Don't throw in the towel, give up or say you can't do it. You can get back on the right track again. Here are some simple steps to take:

- ✓ Stop and be still before God.
- ✓ Confess your sins.
- ✓ Ask for forgiveness.
- ✓ Have a repentant heart.
- ✓ Ask the Holy Spirit for help in this area of your life.
- ✓ Get back up again.
- ✓ Continue walking in the abundant life that God promises to you. He offers it. All you have to do is receive it.
- ✓ Review the "ABC" Chapters of this book and continue to walk out the Born-Again Virgin journey. Don't look back. Just keep moving forward.

✓ Let your accountability partner know what happened. Ask your accountability partner to get more involved in this area that you are struggling with.

If you break any of the boundaries that you have set at any time, repeat the steps above. Each time you do this, you are being transformed from a worldly person to a godly person. Remember it is a process and it will take time. Don't give up and, most importantly, don't turn away from God!

I press on toward the goal to win the prize for which God has called me heavenward in Christ Jesus.

Philippians 3:14

So what do you do when you know you are in over your head with a person and you know you can't get yourself out? The first thing you must do is pray to God for help. Then you must detach yourself from this person. This means no communication at all such as talking, emails, texting, notes, letters, etc. I recommend staying away for at least three months. If you continue with any type of communication with this person, you will not be able to think straight.

If you have been physical with each other, you will have a harder time detaching yourself. Remember, it is not impossible, just difficult. The most important step at this point is getting your accountability partner involved. If you find yourself in this predicament, you probably haven't kept your accountability partner updated on a regular basis.

When you start to do things you know you shouldn't be doing, you might want to isolate from people you know will not approve of the situation. That is why it is important to choose strong and compassionate accountability partners who will understand your struggles but won't let you off too easy. You must keep your accountability partner updated on a regular basis, daily if necessary. I cannot stress enough that without people in your life who will hold you accountable, you will go astray.

Let's take a look at where you are at today - right here, right now. Evaluate yourself with the following questions:

Time-Out #16

1. What is my purpose in life?

    _____

    _____

    _____

    _____

    _____

2. What took me off track from my purpose?

    _____

    _____

    _____

    _____

    _____

3. What do I need to do to get re-focused?

    _____

    _____

    _____

    _____

    _____

4. **What are some things I still need to work on to be ready for a dating/relationship?**

   ➤ _____

       _____

       _____

   ➤ _____

       _____

       _____

   ➤ _____

       _____

       _____

*We wait in hope
for the Lord,
He is our help and
our shield.*
Psalm 33:20

15

GRADUATION

"Moving To The Next Level"

You did it! Just like school, when you pass every test, you are ready to graduate. This does not mean you stop learning, but you are ready to move on to the next level in your journey. Remember how some of you graduated from kindergarten, then elementary school, then to junior high, to high school and off to college you went. But even after you graduated from college, you continued to learn on the job. Learning is a never-ending process in life.

So what does that mean to your Born-Again Virgin education? Congratulations, you have graduated from basic training. You are now ready to move on to the next level. You will continue to move to a higher level as you get closer to God. The Holy Spirit will be your teacher, guide, and counselor. Always remember, you can go back to the basics and review the ABC's in this book if you ever get in a jam. It's always good to go back and review what you learned so it will stay with you throughout your Born-Again Virgin journey. Don't forget to evaluate your progress every quarter to see how you are doing. Just like basic addition, subtraction, multiplication and division in mathematics, the basics you've learned so far will help you in the rest of your journey whether you are single or married.

Let's take a look of what you want to do in life. Do you know your calling in life? What about your passions or dreams? What is it that you have always wanted to do since you were a child? Finish this sentence, "When I grow up, I want to be a _____." That dream may still be there, it just needs to be re-birthed. If you don't know, stop right now and ask God to birth

"Where there is no *vision, the people perish"

Proverbs 29:18 (KJV)

something new into your spirit so you will have direction for your life.

I've counseled women who don't have dreams for their future other than waiting around for a husband, so they can be his helpmate. Guess what? These women are still waiting and sadly are wasting precious time. There is more to life than just waiting around and going through the motions until you get your "big break" with marriage.

Perhaps, you will be a helpmate to a husband someday, but it is still important for you to understand your own dreams and passions. Otherwise, you will experience strife in your marriage. For example, you both may love ministry, however, he may love the adventure of doing foreign missionary work, but you are happy staying in a small town and being involved in a local church.

I am not saying this won't work, but you will spend many nights alone if he is in a foreign country for weeks at a time. And you thought single life was lonely. There are many married women whose husbands' ministries or professions require them to spend more time in hotel beds rather than their own beds at home. This can put a strain on any marriage, especially after the kids come.

Your happiness does not depend on a mate or marriage. You came into this world by yourself and God has a purpose in your life, only for you. Joining up with a mate is a bonus. When God brings your mate into your life, you will compliment each other's purpose in life. Your dreams will not clash but will be knitted together for an even a greater purpose on this earth.

When God brought Mike into my life, I was already walking in my purpose. Just like these women that are still waiting for their husbands, I waited and waited and waited. Then I waited even some more. I thought that God would bring me my mate at the church that I was attending. After all, I was serving in the single's ministry group and I was faithful to the church.

It wasn't until I went on a two-week mission trip to Romania that God birthed a passion in my heart for hurting people. I was ready to go into the foreign mission field and conquer the world for Jesus! I was fired up and when I returned home from the trip, I had such a stirring in my spirit that I was restless for a whole year. I didn't know what I was supposed to do, but I did know that I needed to have a greater purpose in my life.

The Singles group at my church went on another mission trip, but this time to the Los Angeles Dream Center. At that time, I was in a relationship with a new Christian. I felt I needed to let him go and experience a mission trip without my distraction. So I stayed back. The group went again six months later but this time, I had hurt myself and I was on crutches. From both trips, I heard great testimonies from my friends. I knew in my heart that there was something down there I needed to experience.

One of my friends that went on the trip said she would take me down for the weekend. As we got off the freeway, I looked up onto the hill and there stood a huge building. Remember back in Chapter 9, where I talked about the crossroad in my life? When I saw the Dream Center on the hill, something in me said, "Could this be my castle?" This vision came back to me after a couple of years had gone by. I thought that vision was for that situation I was in with that handsome guy, but it was a vision of my future.

As soon as I stepped onto the Dream Center campus, my restless spirit was restless no more. Peace came over me and I knew this was where God wanted me to be. It was an amazing feeling and felt like home.

When I returned from this trip, I started the process of selling my house and possessions so I could re-locate to Los Angeles. I knew my purpose in life was to help people who were in need. One of the reasons I knew Mike was my mate for life is that his purpose in life is similar to mine. He has a heart to help hurting people just like I do. I have become his help-mate and he has helped me with completing my purpose in life.

Our marriage is a bonus because we help each other fulfill our individual dreams. God has also given us new dreams together as a couple. I share this because, like me, you may have gotten too comfortable of where you are at. You need a change. You may not need to do something drastic as I did, but if you are not happy with your life right now, make some changes.

If you are not involved with your church, start volunteering there. There are also many other opportunities such as a local community youth center, sporting venue or maybe even in your own neighborhood. In James 1:27, it says we are to look after orphans and widows. May be there is an elderly lady you know that has a hard time doing things around the house. Volunteer to clean her house or have tea with her once a month. Become a big sister to someone that belongs to the foster care system. There are plenty of foster care children that need a friend and someone to look up to.

Get out there and start changing your life by helping others. Don't wait for your mate to have purpose in your life, instead find your purpose in life now as a Born-Again Virgin. If you are willing to get outside of your comfort zone, God will direct your steps into the life of abundance, joy and contentment. Make a difference in someone else's life and watch God make a difference in your life.

You now have all the basic tools you need to renew your life as a Born-Again Virgin. However, don't stop here. This is just the beginning of what God wants to do on your Born-Again Virgin journey. You can find purity and true fulfillment in this season of singleness. Only you have the power to make this the most exciting, rewarding and satisfying time of your life. Be wise, choose carefully, and enjoy being a Born-Again Virgin!

i accountability. (2009). In *Merriam-Webster Online Dictionary*. Retrieved March 9, 2009, from http://www.merriamwebster.com/dictionary/accountability

Made in the USA
San Bernardino, CA
12 December 2015